DIY Magazine Guide to

UPHOLSTERY

DESMOND GASTON

Illustrated by Tig Sutton

HarperCollins*Publishers*

This edition specially produced for New DIY magazine by
arrangement with HarperCollins*Publishers*
Adapted from *Upholstery: A Practical Guide* by Desmond Gaston.
Please note that figure numbers for chapter seven do not run
sequentially from chapter six.

First published in 1982 by William Collins Sons & Co Ltd
London, Glasgow, Sydney, Auckland, Johannesburg
Reprinted 1983

ISBN 0583 314651

Text set by Advanced Filmsetters (Glasgow) Ltd
Printed and bound in Great Britain by Cox and Wyman, Reading, Berks.

Contents

1 Tools, Equipment and Materials

2 Buying Upholstered Furniture

3 Basic Skills in Upholstery

Complete Work Projects

4 The Drop-In Seat

5 Single Chair with Stuffed-Over Seat

6 Modern Wing Fireside Chair

7 A-Z of Upholstery Snippets

1 Tools, Equipment and Materials

Anyone who takes up the trade of the upholsterer initially has one small advantage over those entering many other trades, in that the hand tools required are comparatively simple and inexpensive. For those of you who are beginners I will list the necessary tools and describe their uses.

As the first task we face when reupholstering is undoing, unpicking and ripping off the old materials, let us start with the instruments of destruction.

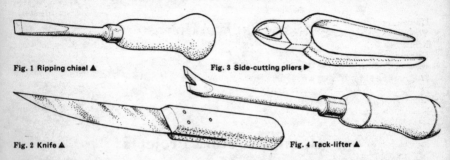

Fig. 1 Ripping chisel ▲   Fig. 3 Side-cutting pliers ▶

Fig. 2 Knife ▲   Fig. 4 Tack-lifter ▲

TOOLS

Ripping Chisel
This is a tool exclusive to the upholsterer. It is used for getting out all the old tacks easily and quickly. I have two, one with a wide blade, the other with a narrow one. The ripping chisel (fig. 1) is used with a small mallet.

Knives
A collection of sharp—and I do mean sharp—knives is essential to enable you to slash away all the old coverings, hessians and twines (fig. 2).

Pair of Pincers
Thinking again about removing tacks—a small pair of pincers is very handy. Try and get some with the jaws ground from the underside with no bevel on the top faces so that they will remove tacks, nails and pins that are close in to the wood.

Side-Cutting Pliers
I have a small pair of side-cutting pliers that I have adapted by grinding the jaws to more

of a point when closed (fig. 3). You would be surprised how useful these are for removing awkward tacks. You can dig the points into the wood round a tack head and extract the tack with ease. I always keep my pliers in my pocket when circulating among students in the class and lend them out for removing wrongly positioned tacks.

Tack-Lifter
This needs to have a well defined crook, as illustrated (fig. 4), and although not a lot of use for removing ordinary tacks, it is essential for extracting the dome-headed decorative chair nails that are frequently used in leather upholstery. And now to tools of construction.

Scissors
These come under both headings, as they are needed for unpicking as well as refurbishing.
Cutting-out shears: these are used for making long, straight cuts in covering cloths, hessians, linings, etc.
Small pointed trimmers: are for small cuts, trimming surplus fabric, fitting upholstery cloth and unpicking.

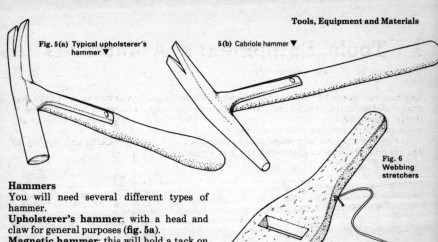

Fig. 5(a) Typical upholsterer's hammer ▼

5(b) Cabriole hammer ▼

Fig. 6 Webbing stretchers

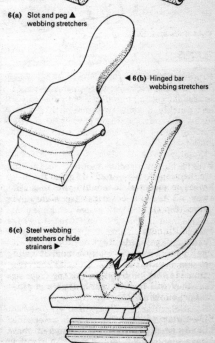

6(a) Slot and peg ▲ webbing stretchers

◀ 6(b) Hinged bar webbing stretchers

6(c) Steel webbing stretchers or hide strainers ▶

Hammers

You will need several different types of hammer.

Upholsterer's hammer: with a head and claw for general purposes (**fig. 5a**).

Magnetic hammer: this will hold a tack on its face, and is useful for those places where fingers cannot reach. It is also invaluable for picking up dropped tacks.

Cabriole hammer: a rare specimen nowadays, this is used for fine tacking work around and near show wood and into tacking rebates where a larger-headed hammer would cause damage to the woodwork (**fig. 5b**).

Two-headed hammer: combines the general purpose with the cabriole but, of course, does not have the very useful claw for removing temporary tacks.

Heavy hammer: I like a slightly heavier, larger-faced hammer to use with large tacks when webbing. With this hammer tacks can be driven well home, a very important point to remember, especially when fastening the webbing.

Webbing Stretchers

There are three types.

Slot and peg: the webbing is pushed down through the slot and the peg inserted in the loop of webbing which protrudes underneath (**fig. 6a**).

Hinged bar: this is the sort I favour. The webbing is looped beneath the bar and the hinge action pinches and grips the webbing (**fig. 6b**).

Pincer-type: these webbing stretchers are also known as wide-jawed hide strainers (**fig. 6c**). They are much more costly and rely upon a hard grip to hold the webbing, but they are useful for short ends of webbing.

Fig. 7 Needles (all drawn approximately half size)

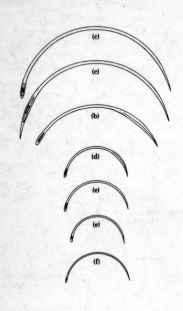

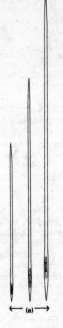

7(a) Mattress needles
7(b) Spring needle
7(c) Semi-circular needles
7(d) Bayonet point needle
7(e) Round point needles
7(f) Cording needle

Needles

The different needles required for sewing with twine are illustrated in **fig. 7a–f**.

Mattress needles: you will need three sizes of these double-pointed needles: a very long one, 350 mm (14 in), 12 gauge thickness; one of medium length, 250 mm (10 in), 13 gauge thickness; and a short one, 180 mm (7 in), 14 gauge thickness (**fig. 7a**).

Spring needle: the slightly curved spring needle has what we call a bayonet point (**fig. 7b**). It is used for sewing or fastening springs to webbing or hessian. You will need one that measures 125 mm (5 in) or 150 mm (6 in).

Semi-circular needles: these are used for sewing with twine. Their size is determined by the length of the needle measured round the curve (**fig. 7c**), and if you can also buy

one with a point at each end, so much the better. If not, you can modify the one-pointed curved needle for a certain type of work, as I will describe later (page 185).

For use with thread or cotton much smaller curved needles are required.

Bayonet point needle: you need one 75 mm (3 in) length, 17 gauge thickness, for use on tough materials such as leather (**fig. 7d**).

Round point needles: for general upholstery work you need one 75 mm (3 in), 17 gauge, and one 60 mm (2½ in), 17 gauge (**fig. 7e**).

Cording needles: get two or three in 75 mm (3 in) length, 19 gauge (**fig. 7f**). These fine needles are used for sewing on decorative chair cord and for sewing on braid and fringe. They tend to break easily but they are not expensive.

Regulators

These instruments (**fig. 8**) have a number of uses—packing and distributing stuffing, marking, and in buttonwork. Also, if you are like me and have rather large fingers, the regulator is very useful as an extra finger for holding covering material while fixing.

Pins and Skewers

Upholsterer's pins and skewers are items unique to the trade. The pins look like dressmakers' pins but are at least 38 mm (1½ in) long. The skewers are 75 mm (3 in) or 100 mm (4 in) long. Pins and skewers are used for temporarily holding and fixing coverings, hessians and in cushion work.

Rules and Measures

Rules, measures and straight edges will all be used in your upholstery work.

Steel tape: the most important measuring tool. Nearly all measurements in upholstery involve distances round and over curved surfaces, so the tape must be flexible.

Yardstick: most of the new yardsticks measure one metre but also include imperial measurements. As well as a yardstick's obvious purpose for measuring or checking lengths of cloth, webbing, hessian and so on, it is very useful for setting out, and as a straight edge.

Upholstery gauge—'Gaston's special': This is a tool that you can make yourself: I designed it to gauge guide lines on the first stuffing upholstery scrim for lines of stitches and ties. It can be cut from wood 2 cm (¾ in) thick, with a small coping saw, fret saw or a band saw. The notches at each end are made with a rat-tail file or cut as Vs with a small saw. In **fig. 9** I have shown the dimensions for this particular gauge which will serve most purposes.

Staple gun

The staple gun is a tool which has proved popular with upholsterers during the last few years and is used a great deal in modern upholstery. However, I hesitate to use staples on antique work, except in certain special circumstances, which I will detail later on. A staple gun is a great time-saver. It can be bought at most hardware stores but, when purchasing one, do take a piece of hardwood

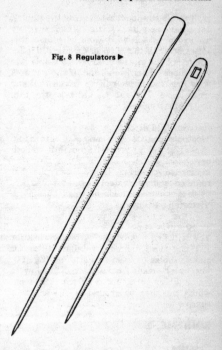

Fig. 8 Regulators ▶

Fig. 9 Gaston's special upholstery gauge ▼

notch for marker

notch for marker

10.25 cm (4″)

3.25 cm (1¼″)

27cm (10⅝″)

2cm (¾″)

with you in your pocket to try out the stapler. Some have very light springs which are of no use except on softwood—and, of course, it is softwood that the shop assistant will offer you to try out this weapon! Fire a staple into your piece of hardwood and, if the gun is a good one, the staple will be driven well and truly home. The gun should take the thin 6 mm ($\frac{1}{4}$ in) staples.

Button-Fold Sticks

'Gaston's specials': you can make button-fold sticks (**fig. 10**) for yourself from thin, smooth hardwood. Being made of wood they are kinder to covering fabric than the flat rounded end of a steel regulator and are used to make the folds between buttons in Victorian buttonwork.

Tubular Cutter

You will find a good use in buttonwork for a 25 mm (1 in) diameter tubular cutter for making holes in foam and stuffing (**fig. 11**). This can be made from a piece of steel cycle frame tubing cut to about 150 mm (6 in) long, which can then be ground at one end to a sharp edge.

EQUIPMENT

Trestles

It is always important for both comfort and efficiency to have your work at the right height, so trestles of different heights are necessary. I have three sizes: a pair of high trestles for working on seats of easy chairs; a medium-size pair for doing arms; and a pair of low ones for working on backs and wings. Each trestle has a groove or trough in the top. This takes the castors and legs, thus preventing the chair or settee from moving while you are working on it.

A Workmate

I have a Workmate that is in constant use and I have made a table top that can be clamped to the top. This is very useful for working on single chair seats or stools, as the legs can be adjusted to two heights. The lower position is used when ripping off, webbing and putting on stuffing, while the higher level makes edge stitching, covering and trimming easier.

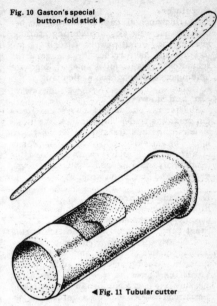

Fig. 10 Gaston's special button-fold stick ▶

◀ Fig. 11 Tubular cutter

Cutting-Out Table

A sheet of 12 mm ($\frac{1}{2}$ in) plywood 2.4 × 1.2 m (8 × 4 ft) screwed to a framework of 25 × 50 mm (1 × 2 in) and set on the top of the high trestles will prove a boon for cutting out, setting out and other table jobs. It will be much more convenient and comfortable than using the floor.

Softening

A builders' word for protective padding or cushioning to help spread the weight load over fragile surfaces. For your softening save some old foam cushions that you can use to rest the backs of easy chairs on when they are inverted for webbing and so on.

MACHINERY

Carding Machine

The carding machine is the upholsterer's most expensive piece of machinery, but it is not so necessary for an amateur as, these days, you can buy ready-carded stuffings and fillings—at a price. However, if you intend to do a fair bit of upholstery and you spot an old carding machine in a sale or junk yard, buy it—that is, if you have room to set it up, for it needs a shed of its own. It will soon pay for itself. Another idea is to get together a group of people as keen on upholstery as yourself, and set up a carding and machining centre in someone's garden shed. You can all take your stuffings there and rejuvenate them, for that is what a carding machine does. The lumps of matted horsehair or other types of filling are fed into a hopper and passed between opposing spiked rollers which separate and comb the fibres while all the dust is sucked out by an extractor fan at the back. The filling then comes out all clean, soft and springy, ready to be re-used. If you cannot get access to a carding machine, the other alternative is to get to know your friendly neighbourhood upholsterer, who, for a fee, may do your carding for you.

Sewing Machine

This is the next largest piece of machinery. You can probably get by with an ordinary domestic model to begin with, but this will not deal with the very heavy fabrics, such as tapestry and thick modern leathercloths.

These may have to be fed through in four or more thicknesses when making piped cushion covers, for example. Later on you may be able to purchase second-hand a tailor's or industrial sewing machine but meanwhile if you have to manage with your domestic machine fit it with the thickest gauge needle it will take.

Button Presses

I mention these in passing just in case you see any for sale second-hand, perhaps in an auction sale. Since most people would never be able to guess their purpose, you might be able to buy them cheaply. They can be bought new, but they are quite expensive now—however, again, perhaps they could be acquired by your upholstery group for a joint machining centre. There are two types of press.

Cutting press: the cutting press (fig. 12a) has as accessories circular cutters to cut discs of cloth for covering button moulds.

Fly press: this press (fig. 12b) can be fitted with appropriate dies and when operated it compresses a disc of covering material and a two-part button mould together. In this way it makes an upholstery button very quickly and easily.

Fig. 12
Button presses

12(a) Press for cutting
   button covers ▶

12(b) Fly button-making
   press with
   two-piece die ▶

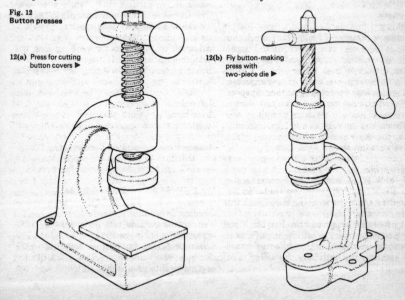

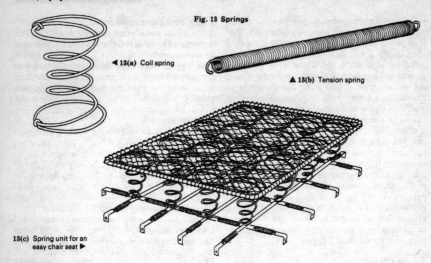

Fig. 13 Springs

◀ 13(a) Coil spring

▲ 13(b) Tension spring

13(c) Spring unit for an
easy chair seat ▶

MATERIALS

Let us look at the materials and sundries used in upholstery, some of which, if you are tackling a number of jobs, might to advantage be bought in quantity.

Supports

Webbing: I find the best and longest lasting webbing is English 50 mm (2 in) black and white. It pays always to use the best, because webbing is a basic support and it needs to be strong enough to bear the weight of springs or filling, which are sometimes compressed by large persons descending on them at speed. **Rubber webbing**: many modern upholstered chairs have rubber webbing for their seat platforms and usually this is 50 mm (2 in) in width. Rubber webbing makes a comfortable and efficient base for a cushioned seat but will need replacing after three to five years of use. When buying rubber webbing get a good thick type—they do vary considerably in quality. Metal clips are supplied for fastening to the ends of the webbing straps, and this makes for easier fixing.

Heavy hessian or tarpaulin: is a thick and strong hessian and you will be using this as a platform over webbing or to cover upholstery springs. I usually buy the 450 g (16 oz) tarpaulin.

Springs

There are three main forms as illustrated: **Upholstery coil spring**: is the most common and the earliest type of spring. The form of these springs has changed little since the early nineteenth century when they were first introduced into upholstery (fig. 13a). **Tension spring**: is used mostly in seats of fireside chairs. These springs (fig. 13b) are attached to the frame by webbing with eyelets, rings or hardened steel pins. **Spring units**: modern spring unit assemblies for seats (fig. 13c), backs and arms can be obtained in many sizes. The best seat units have small tension springs between the steel base laths and the frame, and have a woven mesh top covering and holding the springs.

Other Hessian and Undercovering Cloth

In addition to tarpaulin hessian there are other lighter-weight hessians. For first stuffing coverings you will need a strong scrim hessian, which is a very pliable canvas for forming edge shapes. Then 280 g (10 oz) hessian is used for bottom coverings and for reinforcing outside arm and back panels. A cheap but strong black cotton lining is sometimes preferred for bottom covering, while for upholstery undercoverings you will need a good quality unbleached calico.

Twines, Cords and Threads

(a) **Laid cord** is the name in the trade for a thickish cord, usually made from hemp or jute. This is used for lacing upholstery springs together.

(b) **Twine**: the stoutest twine, usually called **No. 1**, is used for tying springs to webbing and hessian, and for fastening tufts or buttons. **No. 2** and **No. 3** are finer twines used for edge stitching and for sewing hessians. Keep a lump of beeswax with your twines and use it to dress them. This will preserve and strengthen them.

Nylon tufting twine: nylon twine is the best cord to use for buttonwork. It is expensive but very strong.

Cotton piping cords: the two sizes that I use are the 6 mm ($\frac{1}{4}$ in) for making piping for large proportioned upholstery and a thinner cord 4 mm ($\frac{1}{8}$ in) wide for fine work on smaller chairs and cushions.

Threads and cottons: for ladder or slip stitching two sizes of thread are needed. **No. 18** is a stout thread and **No. 25** a thinner one. I find a **No. 24** cotton is the best general purpose thread for the sewing machine but there are available many nylon and other man-made yarns which are very strong and are suitable for stitching nylon and other cloths made of man-made fibres.

Tacks

There are two varieties in most sizes of upholstery tack. The stouter tack with a large head is called 'improved' and those with smaller heads are called 'fine'. All these are termed 'cut tacks' and are available from hardware stores in 500 g (just over 1 lb) packets. There is another kind called 'bayonet' tacks but these are little used by upholsterers as they are more akin to nails, with square, parallel shanks, (**fig. 14**).

16 mm ($\frac{5}{8}$ in) improved tacks: the largest tacks, used mostly for fastening webbing.

16 mm ($\frac{5}{8}$ in) fine tacks: can be used for fastening webbing and heavy support hessian when the wood of the frame is liable to split if stouter tacks are used.

13 mm ($\frac{1}{2}$ in) improved tacks: used for fastening support hessians.

13 mm ($\frac{1}{2}$ in) fine tacks: for general tacking through thick covering cloth or multi-thicknesses of cloth.

10 mm ($\frac{3}{8}$ in) fine tacks: the smallest generally used in upholstery, although 6 mm ($\frac{1}{4}$ in) tacks can be obtained for especially delicate work.

Gimp pins: like very fine tacks. They are not merely for fixing gimp or braid but are also useful for general tacking purposes on delicate woodwork. These come in japanned black, white and various colours. Black are the most useful.

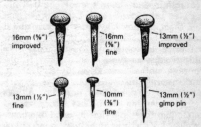

Fig. 14 Tacks and gimp pins

Adhesives

There are two fields in upholstery where adhesives are used. An impact adhesive is used for joining and building up rubber and plastic foam. This is not quite the same adhesive as that used for fixing plastic laminates—it is modified to give a soft bond—so that when it is used to join pieces of foam, say to make up a shaped cushion, hard ridges of dried adhesive will not form along the joins. Another type of impact adhesive is used for fastening braids and trimmings. The impact fastness of this glue is retarded so that trimmings can be adjusted before they become firmly fixed. The adhesive is also thixotropic (jelly-like) for easy application.

Fillings

You will learn most about upholstery filling or stuffings when you are stripping and ripping off your chair, settee or couch but I will try to give you a guide to help you recognize the various substances, so that you will know which to save or discard. Let us start with the types of filling to throw away or discard; by the way, most are good to put on your compost heap.

In some poorly upholstered chairs you will find woodwool (shavings) or 'best Italian hair', as it is known to the trade. Then there is brown seaweed and where this has been used as a first stuffing the salt that it contains usually causes the springs to rust through the hessian covering them. Flock is made of old woollen clothes carded up, and mill puff or mill seed is a whitish cotton stuffing resembling cold rice pudding. When this is used it makes a real pudding of a seat—hard and ungiving. Now for the ones that you can save and re-card.

Horsehair and sheep's wool: the best fillings, so take great care of them when you find them, for nowadays they are rare and if you should be lucky enough to find them new the price is prohibitive. Treat animal fibre fillings such as these with a spray to discourage moths. Several of the students in our evening institute class have experimented by washing their horsehair fillings before re-carding them. They either washed small quantities at a time by hand in a bowl, or placed the hair in an old but sound pillow case and washed it in a washing machine. Do be careful if you try this, though, for I shudder to think what would happen to the machine if the hair should escape. I must say that, although the process seems laborious, the resulting super-clean, sweet-smelling horsehair is a joy to work with.

Vegetable fibres: there are vegetable fibres worth saving too, among them Algerian fibre, a curly grass-like filling, usually green or black in colour, and coconut fibre, also known as coir fibre. Both are very durable stuffings and can be re-carded successfully. However, if they show signs of becoming dry, brittle and short, they are best thrown out or burnt. Cotton and wool-and-cotton felt fillings can also be re-carded and used as top stuffings.

Upholstery foam: polyether plastic foam can be obtained in thicknesses from 6 mm ($\frac{1}{4}$ in) to 100 mm (4 in). Where possible, for the sake of safety try to obtain flame-retardant foam. For cushion interiors I use rubber block foam, 50 mm (2 in), 75 mm (3 in) or 100 mm (4 in) thickness. This has more resilience than the plastic variety, and lasts longer.

Waddings, felts, acrylic wool: upholstery is rather like road building—the coarser stuff goes underneath and is topped by something finer to make a smooth and even surface. To get the smoother, softer surface we need cotton wadding. Here again, buy the best quality, which should have been manufactured evenly with none of the lumps or foreign bodies that are frequently found in cheaper wadding. It comes in 10 m (33 ft) rolls and is about 48 cm (19 in) in width, but the best quality wadding can be split or opened up still further, giving a thickness of wadding which will then be about 90 cm (36 in) wide.

Rolls of white cotton felt or wool-and-cotton mixtures can be obtained in sheet form up to 25 mm (1 in) thick. This is useful for top filling as it remains soft and does not consolidate too much.

If you want to add even more richness to the feel of your upholstery, acrylic wool is good. This again comes in rolls, and in various thicknesses but it is much more expensive than the vegetable waddings.

Coverings (Furnishing Fabrics)

Upholstery covering materials are many and varied, some cheap, some expensive and, as with everything, you pay the most for the best quality cloth. I will list the names of the different cloths that you are most likely to come across and try to describe them but if you want to become familiar with the various weaves my advice is that you try to visit as many fabric shops as you can and study, feel and compare the different cloths at close quarters. Also study the different fibres that go into the make-up of each cloth.

To my mind, cloths that contain real wool are definitely the most durable but many man-made fibres are strong, soft and wear well.

Tapestry: the best is made of wool or a cotton and wool mixture and a good quality tapestry is a very durable, thick, closely woven cloth. It is made in both traditional and modern designs.

Quilted tapestry: the cloth is woven in two layers which are then interwove.. at places in the design, to give an embossed look.

Brocatelle: this is a type of brocade cloth with a design woven in relief using both glossy and dull yarns to highlight or shade the pattern.

Damask: many damasks are plain one-colour cloths with the design created by clever changes in the weaving. You will probably remember grandmother's beautiful white damask table cloths. There are also striped damasks, such as those in Regency stripe.

Cotton velour: is a type of velvet with a very closely woven cotton pile. It has a rich, luxurious look, but some 'shade' badly after a little use, especially on chair seats.

Dralon velvet: this ever-popular furnishing fabric now comes in many textures and finishes from a bright sheen to a dull suede leather look. There are dralon velvets in ribbed pile, corduroy, slub pile and some with beautifully embossed and colourful patterns. Dralon is a very durable, easy-to-clean cloth.

Mohair velvet: this usually has a shaggy look but is lovely and soft to touch.

Real velvet: there is nothing to rival the look and the feel of real silk velvet. But what a price!

Uncut moquette: this tends to be derided nowadays and brings to mind old railway carriage upholstery. Nevertheless, made in 100 per cent wool it is a most durable fabric.

Tweeds: these have burst upon the market in recent years in many forms and designs and are good value when closely woven and substantial. Tweeds are made up in many of the man-made fibres but the best are the pure wool tweeds.

Leathercloths: these are now a far cry from the early oil cloth imitation leathers. There are a variety of different grains and effects available and they are often difficult to tell from real leather.

These are just a few of the large variety of furnishing fabrics available; there are many more for your choice. Choose carefully because quality is important so try to learn how to recognize good cloths by their feel, their weight, their texture and the closeness of the weave (hold them up to the light).

For instructions on measuring fabric refer to the sections on pages 27 and 91.

Trimmings

To finish this chapter I will illustrate a few of the popular trimmings used to give a good finish to upholstery work (fig. 15a–n). I'm afraid however, that these names are not universally used and sometimes trimmings are given different names. Banding and studs, *Hidem* piping and *Flexibead* trimmings are for leatherwork only.

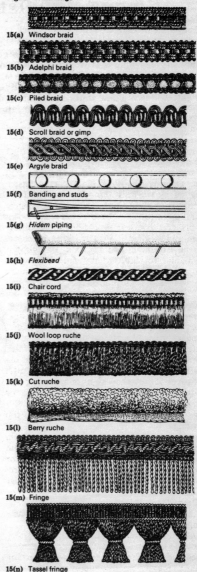

Fig. 15 Trimmings

15(a) Windsor braid

15(b) Adelphi braid

15(c) Piled braid

15(d) Scroll braid or gimp

15(e) Argyle braid

15(f) Banding and studs

15(g) *Hidem* piping

15(h) *Flexibead*

15(i) Chair cord

15(j) Wool loop ruche

15(k) Cut ruche

15(l) Berry ruche

15(m) Fringe

15(n) Tassel fringe

2 Buying Upholstered Furniture

It is no easy task when looking at upholstered furniture to tell good quality from bad, because everything is stuffed over and covered up; and so the unwary often end up buying a 'pig in a poke' and paying large sums of money for nothing but a very poorly made frame. Experience is dearly bought in this field so I thought it might be useful if I jotted down a few hints, pointers and guides to help when you go hunting in sale-rooms or junk shops for those bargains.

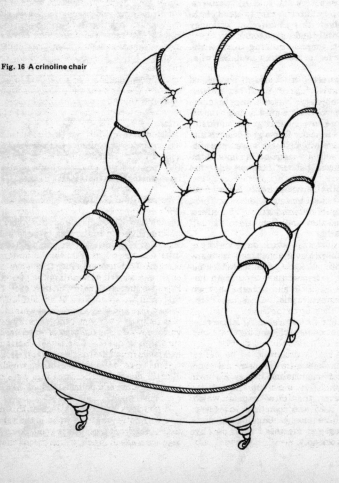

Fig. 16 A crinoline chair

WHAT TO LOOK FOR

You can get caught out so easily. Someone I know came to me with a wing easy chair that he had just bought. When I first set eyes on it I was puzzled—there was something about it that did not ring true. It certainly looked old if one could go by the leg assembly, which was mahogany with stretchers between square section legs, and seemed to date from the 1760s. But the upholstered top part seemed a little unbalanced somehow. The shape of the wings had more than a hint of years later than 1760. So, with my curiosity stirred, I stripped the chair of its upholstery. My suspicions were well founded, for I discovered that this was a two-in-one chair. Yes, I reckon the legs and stretchers were early but a cleverly adapted frame, probably of a chair dating from about 1830, had been set on top. This was not all, because it was clear that the wings and the scroll arm fronts had pieces of even newer wood added to alter their shape. It always amazes me the lengths to which some people will go in order to deceive, but may be I am being uncharitable for it could be that originally it just seemed a good idea to make two wrecks into one useful chair. However, although the original intention may have been honourable, a chair like this is not what it seems and so the moral of the story is that you must look carefully and suspiciously at old pieces of furniture and examine them well before paying out large sums of money.

You will, of course, ask how you can examine furniture thoroughly when everything is covered with upholstery. I think I can help you here: let's take a walk around an imaginary antique shop and pretend that we want to buy an easy chair.

Examining the Frame

Now, here is a comfortable-looking chair, one that we call a Crinoline chair (fig. 16).

Some say the chairs came to be called Crinoline chairs because they were designed for ladies wearing crinoline dresses. My own theory is that the term crinoline is perhaps related to the construction of the chair, which is made with a hoop iron and rod upper structure built upon a circular or part-circular wooden seat frame with legs. This construction reminds me of the hooped support for a crinoline skirt.

Some chairs of the same shape are made with wooden frames, now how can we tell the difference when everything is covered? You can usually feel if it is wood if you press your hand into the top or sides of the back, but a more reliable way of checking is to take hold of the top of the chair as you face it from the front, hold the seat front with your other hand and gently pull the back forward. If the frame is iron there will be considerable give here as the iron rod and hoop frame bends under your gentle pressure. A wooden frame should be firm and unmoving. I say, should be, because with this test you can also tell the state of the frame and if you hear creaks and groans when you pull, then this indicates that the joints are loose or broken. Or, in the case of an iron frame, if you find too much movement here or a decided looseness between the back and the arms, this probably indicates that the ironwork has broken; this most often occurs where the back meets the arms.

Before I go any further, let me say that you will probably give offence to the owner of the shop if you go round pulling his chairs about. But these tests can be done quite gently and unobtrusively, so that no one notices.

Signs of Good Quality

Let's move over to the easy chair in the corner; this is completely stuffed over, with nothing showing in the way of wood but the legs (fig. 17). However, we can deduce a lot from just these legs. Firstly, the design and turning of the legs are clues to the age of the chair but, as well as denoting the period, the legs also indicate quality or lack of it. Now, this chair we are looking at has elegant, well turned legs and they are made of walnut.

It helps a lot if you can get to know the various woods, for the type of wood used is a sure sign of quality. The better chairs have legs made from hardwoods such as mahogany, walnut, oak or the finer birch wood. On cheaper chairs beech-turned legs were often used, coloured and polished to look like more expensive wood.

If you look at the back legs of this chair you will notice that the wood is the same as that of the front legs; this is good. Some back legs are made of beech, which means that the

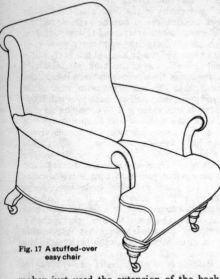

Fig. 17 A stuffed-over
easy chair

maker just used the extension of the back upright of the chair and did not take the trouble to join on the hardwood for the legs. The shape of the back legs is important too; you will notice that these have a well defined curve. Examine the castors; a proud manufacturer would always fit the legs with good quality brass castors with brass or porcelain bowls—but check that they are the originals. You can do this by inspecting the screws that fasten the castors to the legs to see if they have been disturbed or if there are any new screw holes.

It is also a good idea to examine—surreptitiously—the size of the wood of the frame, especially the seat frame; just place your hand under one side of the bottom and judge the size of the wood here. It should be at least 45 to 50 mm (1¾ to 2 in) square in section, for this is where the strength of the frame needs to be.

Now the chair may look bonny, and you have established that it is of good quality, but I wonder what state the frame is in? There are a couple of tests that you can do to tell if all is well here. Face the chair and take hold of the left-hand side of the top of the back and the right arm front, then gently pull diagon-

ally; do the same with the opposite corners and, if there is a lot of movement, this means that the frame joints are loose. Place your hands on the arms and pull these towards each other and you can then tell whether the joints here are loose or not.

Examining for Woodworm
One question that is difficult to answer is, whether there is any woodworm in the frame inside? Woodworm in the confines of the inside of an easy chair can spread rampantly with very little, if any, signs from the outside that anything is amiss, especially if the legs are of mahogany, which woodworm does not often attack. On the chair that we are looking at the walnut legs would most probably show signs of infestation—just one or two holes could mean that the inside was riddled. If woodworm had been making a real meal of the frame, then the frame test described earlier should give an indication of this.

Let us leave the antique shop and make our way to the local auction sales-rooms. It is viewing day and you will be allowed much more freedom to examine the merchandise thoroughly. This is the best place to buy a chair or other upholstered furniture if you want to refurbish it yourself. In antique shops every piece will be reupholstered or smartened up to look good, but inside you will often find just the old upholstery plus a lot of wadding which has been added to fill up hollows in the seat and back and the whole lot has been covered with new material. All this is done as cheaply as possible for a quick sale. I hasten to add that not all antique shops sell goods of this description; some have reputable craftsmen to do their upholstery.

POINTS TO LOOK FOR IN A VICTORIAN SPOONBACK CHAIR
A Victorian spoonback chair catches your eye in the sales-room. That will fetch a good price, I bet. But is it of good quality? There is a lot more to see on a chair like this, with so much wood on show (**fig. 18**). You can do the usual tests for the robustness of the frame and joints. Observe the sweep of the moulded show wood round the back, is it evenly curving and do the two sides match? If the chair is carved, you can look for delicacy of carving.

Fig. 18 A Victorian
spoon-back chair

The front legs and front facing wood to the arms should be elegantly turned or carved. The size and appearance of the back legs are good indicators of quality. The back legs of the best chairs will have a well defined curved or ogee (double curved) shape, and will be about 50 mm (2 in) square in section. The legs on poorer chairs look skimpy and weak.

Checking for Bad Repairs

The wood, be it mahogany, oak, walnut, satinwood or satin birch, should be examined for splits and for bad repairs, such as nails or screws driven through joints. Look at the tops of the front legs; if there are any large holes filled with wax filler, the filler probably conceals a large screw—which could be the only thing holding a front joint together. Look in the vicinity of joints for smaller holes which have been disguised with filler or wax. They could indicate nails that have been punched in and filled over and in this case it will be difficult to dismantle the joint without causing damage to the woodwork.

Fig. 19 A high quality Victorian couch

LOOKING AT COUCHES

The forms and shapes of the Victorian couch or chaise-longue are many and varied. Here are two in the sales-room, and how convenient for us, they are side by side so we will be able to compare them. They are of about the same period but at opposite ends of the scale of quality. One (**fig. 19**), in mahogany, has smooth and exactly carved show wood on the front scroll of the head, surrounding the back and in the form of moulding all round the seat. If we look at the legs, there is plenty of wood in them but they have been delicately turned to give them an elegant look. And they are set off really well with solid brass cup castors. The show wood has been deeply and crisply carved and the polish, although well worn, still has a bit of a shine to it.

Its sale-room neighbour is very different. This couch (**fig. 20**) also has a lot of show wood, but it is of rather dingy walnut—or could it be birch or beech? It is difficult to tell, because the wood has obviously been

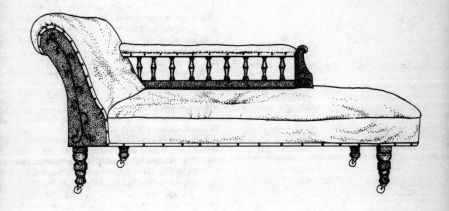

Fig. 20 A couch of inferior quality

varnished and the varnish has perished, cracked and blistered. The show wood facing on the head front is flat and the carving not much more than scratched in. The back consists of a row of turned spindles, each one just slightly different in shape from its neighbour, and topped by a long upholstered pad. No moulded show wood round the seat on this one, although I suspect that at one time there was some but it has fallen off or broken. The last covering has been taken right down to the bottom. But oh dear, the legs . . . not much imagination or art in these! The poor things are only half the thickness they should be to lend a good balance of design to the whole; and the castors are small cast iron and red china sort.

So there you have the good and the bad in a simple Victorian couch. There are many types, forms and designs of couch but I hope that the description of these two will start you looking in detail at all those you come across.

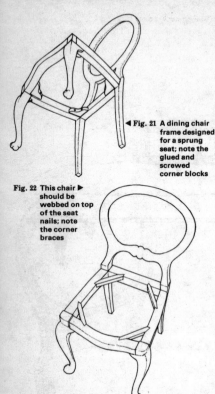

◄ Fig. 21 A dining chair frame designed for a sprung seat; note the glued and screwed corner blocks

Fig. 22 This chair ► should be webbed on top of the seat nails; note the corner braces

DINING CHAIRS

Over there is a set of Victorian dining chairs with balloon backs and stuffed-over seats, shall we have a look at those? The first thing to do when examining a chair is to turn the chair upside down and look at the bottom of the seat. These chairs have no springs in the seats and yet they have a black lining covering the bottom. This is most suspicious, for whoever last upholstered these chairs seems to have had something to hide. Ah, here is one of the set with the bottom lining half off, so let's have a peep inside. Just as I thought, the seat rails are so full of woodworm that pieces are dropping off. We can now see that this seat originally had springs—there are all the tack holes where the webbing had

been fastened on the underside of the rails. Another indication of a sprung seat is the glued and screwed corner blocks (fig. 21). A stuffed-over seat intended to be just top-stuffed without springs would have corner braces notched into the rails in order to give the rails the corner strength needed when webbing was stretched across the top of the seat frame (fig. 22). With this chair we are looking at, obviously the upholsterer could not fix the webbing to the underside because the wood there had perished under the ravages of the woodworm, so he top-webbed it, doing away with the springs, and covering up this awful mess, saying to himself, what the eye doesn't see, etc.

But here is a completely different story . . . When viewing Victorian furniture, you must not only have eyes for the better class things; many of the less expensive pieces are well worth considering, even if they look total wrecks. If you have an eye open you can spot pieces that, with a lot of care, can be brought back to serve a useful existence and look quite beautiful again. In fact, some chairs can be made to look far better than they did when they were new. This brings to mind the two little Victorian servants' hall balloon back chairs that Flora found (fig. 23).

For several years Flora has been an ardent student, not only of upholstery but also of furniture restoration. I looked with a very cynical eye at these two white-painted chairs with greasy, threadbare leathercloth seats which were shedding awful dirty grey flock through several large rents. But despite my expression of doubt, she set to work, taking off the terrible upholstery and with great patience stripping off all the layers of paint. One seat frame had to be renewed—it was too full of woodworm—and we found a nice piece of hornbeam for this. But what an amazing revelation when all the paint was off, for the wood, an attractively grained birch, came up beautifully under Flora's skilful French polishing. After reupholstering, the little banjo-shaped seats, built up this time with proper stitched roll edges and covered in a delicate blue velvet, looked really expensive. So here are two chairs that began life rather humbly, but with a bit of love and care have now become objects of beauty as well as usefulness.

Fig. 23 A Victorian balloon-back chair

◀ 23(a) Before

23(b) After ▶

3   Basic Skills in Upholstery

In this chapter I intend to describe the techniques and methods that are common to most upholstery jobs. I hope that you will then be able to use the chapter like a pocket book of upholstery; something that you can constantly refer back to when tackling different work projects in order to refresh your memory on such basic subjects as knots, fixing webbing, which hessians to use, and so on.

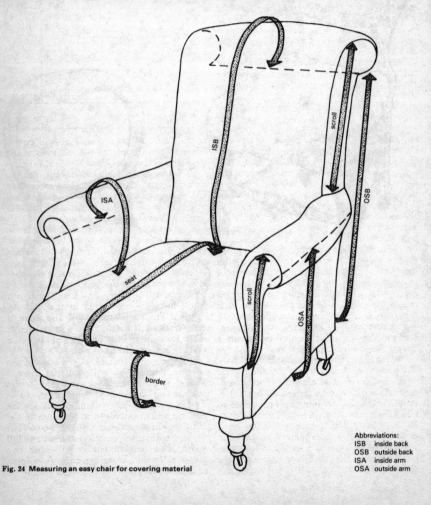

Fig. 24 Measuring an easy chair for covering material

Abbreviations:
ISB   inside back
OSB   outside back
ISA   inside arm
OSA   outside arm

MEASURING UP FOR THE NEW COVERING MATERIAL

Let us imagine that you have in front of you an easy chair of about 1900 vintage (fig. 24)—a chair that has an excellent frame and originally had very good upholstery.

So there you stand viewing this poor old chair all in rags and tatters and I know you are itching to rip off all the old upholstery, but hold on a while. The first thing to do is to measure up for your new covering material while there is still some semblance of shape to the chair. So get your flexible spring steel rule and begin drawing out a table (fig. 25) on which to jot down your measurements.

Before starting to measure, check the way the material should run. With a patterned cloth it is usually easy to see the top and bottom of the design, although some are pretty obscure. Some flowery designs are difficult, but remember, buds at the top, stalks at the bottom. With piled fabrics, such as velvet, the pile or nap should always run downwards. On the arms and inside back it should run down towards the seat; on the seat it should run from back to front. The direction of the pile for the other cuts is obvious.

Most furnishing fabrics are made 132 to 137 cm (52 to 54 in) in width. Your upholstery will be fuller than it is at present so in all your measurements make allowance for this by holding the tape a little away from the present surface. Now, begin by measuring the inside back of the chair; measure the width to determine whether a half width will reach across. On the chair depicted it will, which means that the inside and the outside back coverings will both come from one complete width, so those two headings can be bracketed together and whichever measurement is the greater entered against them.

On this chair the inside arms also take only half a width each, but on a larger chair a full width may have to be allowed for each arm. Any off-cuts should be noted. Do not entertain the thought of joining arm coverings to make them wide enough—some upholsterers do, but this practice does not make for a good job and very little material is saved in the process. When you are taking your arm measurements, tuck your tape well down into the seat side crevice, so that it touches the

Fig. 25 Chart for measuring covering material

Cut	Length	Off cuts	
		Length	Width
inside back			
outside back			
inside arms			
outside arms			
seat			
front border			
cushion			
scroll fronts			
piping			
Total			

tacking bar. Allow a couple of centimetres beyond this. Under the top roll-over of the back and of the arms allow 25 mm (1 in) more than where the outside panel joins. For the outside arms, allow 50 mm (2 in) more than the exact measurement. Here again, a full width may be necessary for each outside arm—if so, note down the off-cuts.

Then measure the seat from back to front. Tuck your tape well into the back crevice, and at the front, allow for the fact that this old seat front has been pushed back considerably through years of use and also that it is nowhere near the height that it should be. There will be nearly half a width left over from the seat—enter this in the 'off-cuts' column. The seat border will also have to come from a full width; for this measurement allow for turning in at the top and plenty for tacking beneath the front rail.

It is time now to look at the sizes of the off-cuts. I think you will find that there is enough to cover the front arm scroll facings and the two scrolls on each side of the back. The rest will do for making piping for the cushion and the scrollwork. Measure for the cushion, allowing 25 mm (1 in) for seams. The top and bottom panels will cut from one full width. The cushion border will need two pieces, full width, to the measure of the depth of the cushion plus 25 mm (1 in) for seams.

Fig. 26 Using the ripping chisel

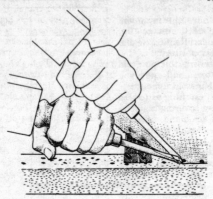

Allowing for Pattern Matching

If your material has a design that needs continuity, you should allow an extra 50 cm (20 in). If you choose a material with a large pattern that necessitates keeping the design central on the back, seat and arms, then you will have to make an extra allowance. Most pattern books show the distance of the repeat of the design, or if you buy from the roll you can get the shop assistant to tell you, or measure for yourself. Usually 75 cm (just under 30 in) is an adequate allowance.

RIPPING OFF

Ripping off is the trade term for taking off the old material and upholstery from the frame. Not much skill in this, you say? Perhaps you are right, but I can endeavour to make this rather boring job more interesting and speedy by pointing out the best ways of doing it.

The tools you will need are a sharp knife and some scissors, a ripping chisel, a small mallet and side-cutting pliers (adapted).

Stripping and Observing

Cut away the covering and remove the filling with your knife and scissors. When I am stripping a chair I like to cut away most of the old hessian, webbing, twines and ties at once, to give easier access to the ripping chisel, but when you are beginning, my advice is to take everything off layer by layer, for you can learn a lot from the old

work. It can be quite exciting when you remove the seat from an old chair such as this one; who knows what treasures you may find among the buttons, tiddlywinks, mottoes from long-pulled Christmas crackers, hairgrips, mouldy nuts and picture postcards of the old chain pier at Brighton. As well as 'treasures' there will be a terrible amount of dust and dirt, so do wear a mask.

Using the Ripping Chisel

The ripping chisel, used with a small mallet, considerably speeds the process of removing tacks, but you must take care with this tool, or you may damage the woodwork. Place the blade of the chisel against a tack head and drive with your mallet. As the tack begins to lift lower the handle of the chisel and continue to drive, but more gently, to remove the tack (**fig. 26**). Keep your eye on the tack being removed and not on the handle of the chisel, but do not hold your face directly over the work—tacks can fly up, and sometimes the heads come off as well. Try to rip in the direction of the grain of the wood to avoid too much damage. Inevitably you will split some pieces from the frame, do save these fragments and stick them back immediately. You will soon get into the swing with your ripping chisel and mallet, but use the adapted side-cutting pliers to clear the tacks from delicate woodwork, such as the wood near the front leg joints of this easy chair.

FIXING WEBBING

Now we turn to the skills involved in re-upholstering. Webbing forms the most important basic support. The illustrations in **fig. 27** show how it should be attached.

Make a 25 mm (1 in) fold at the end of the webbing and place it on the frame with the fold uppermost (**a**).

Fix the webbing to the frame with a staggered row of tacks (**b**). You will have to use your discretion as to the size and number of tacks. For most woods four 15 mm ($\frac{5}{8}$ in) improved tacks will be about right, but a very hard wood may need only 12 mm ($\frac{1}{2}$ in) improved tacks. If the wood splits easily fine tacks will have to be used and, since the fine tacks have smaller heads, more tacks will be required in the row. Be careful how you drive in your tacks. Each should be driven home

with the head perfectly flat and level with the surface of the frame. If a tack is driven in crooked, part of the head will cut into the webbing, weakening the fixing. The whole idea of a large-headed tack is to give the maximum frictional surface between wood, webbing and the tack head.

Figs (**c**) and (**d**) show two different types of webbing stretcher in use—a hinged bar stretcher in (**c**) and a slot and peg stretcher in (**d**). You can see how webbing is held and pulled tight on the different models. Black and white cotton webbing has little elasticity and should not be overstrained. Stretch the webbing and fasten at the stretched end with three tacks. Cut off 25 mm (1 in) from the row of tacks and fold it back. A further two tacks are placed between the three tacks underneath to hold the fold down.

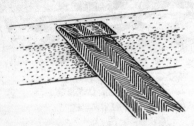

27(a) Folding the webbing over ▶

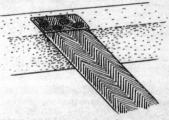

27(b) Four tacks in a staggered row ▲

27(c) Using a hinged bar webbing stretcher ▼

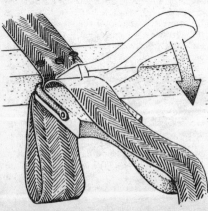

27(d) Using a slot and peg webbing stretcher ▼

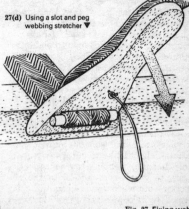

Fig. 27 Fixing webbing

Fig. 28 A quick way of webbing

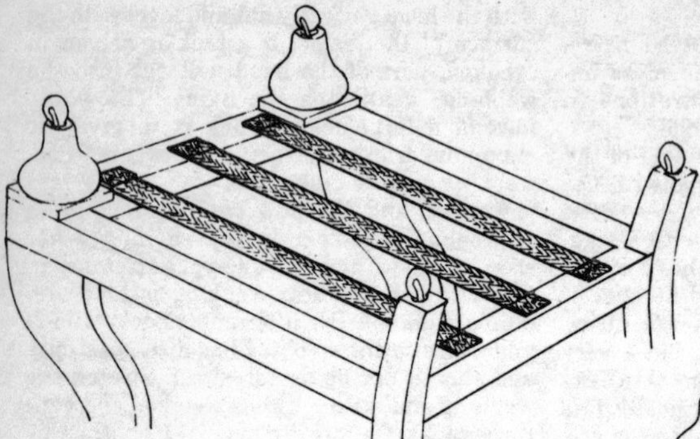

▲ 28(a) Three webs from back to front

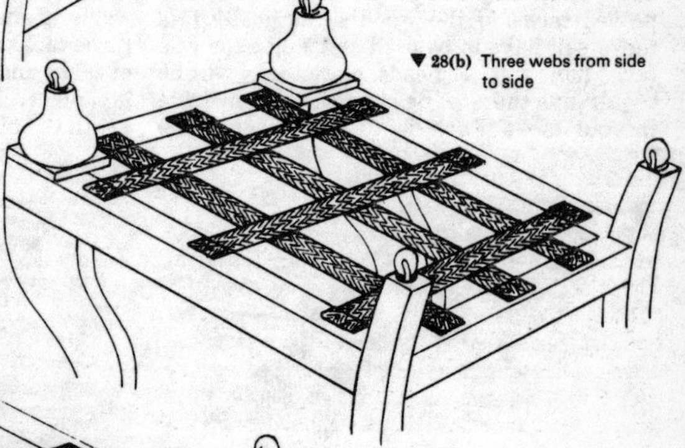

▼ 28(b) Three webs from side to side

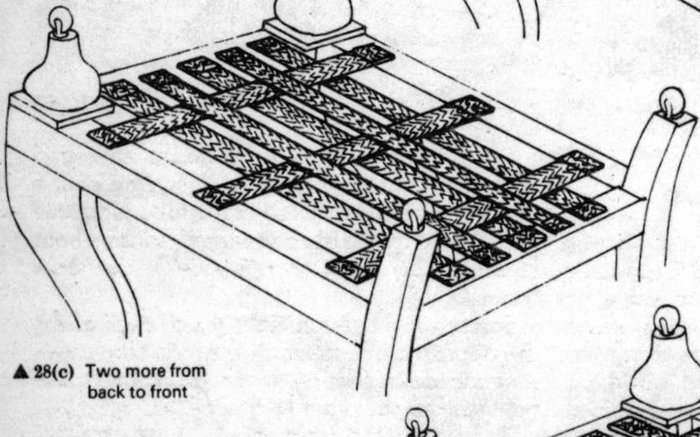

▲ 28(c) Two more from back to front

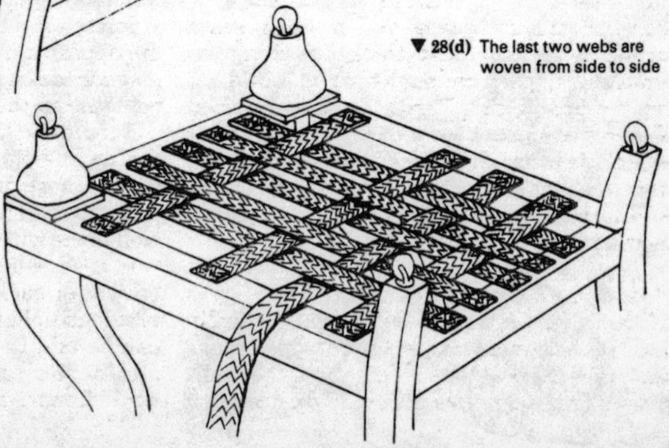

▼ 28(d) The last two webs are woven from side to side

A Quick Way of Webbing

Most people find it easier to stretch and fasten all the webs from back to front and then weave the cross webs in afterwards. But there is a much quicker way of webbing that professional upholsters use and we will employ this method on our easy chair (**fig. 28**). Start by stretching three pieces from back to front as shown in (**a**). Place three more across from side to side and on top of the first webs (**b**). On top of these stretch two more pieces from back to front, between the first three (**c**). The remaining two webs, which are passed across from side to side, are the only ones that are actually woven, through the back-to-front webs (**d**).

The Use of Glue

Some seat frames present a problem when it comes to renewing the webbing. Take, for instance, an occasional chair with a pin cushion seat where there is very little width of wood for fastening webbing—let alone the hessian, undercover and covering material which all have to follow. To add to the difficulties, the seat has probably been re-upholstered once or twice before and there are a multitude of old tack holes. In cases like this I like to squeeze a line of P.V.A. glue from one of those small plastic bottles with a pointed nozzle and tack down the webbing on this, using finer tacks. This gives a much greater hold to the fixing.

Using Heavy Hessian

Next in strength to webbing for upholstery supports is the heavyweight hessian, the 450 g (16 oz) tarpaulin. On loose drop-in seats or top-webbed stuffed-over dining chair seats tarpaulin is fixed next to the webbing, to complete a platform on which to build up further upholstery. Tarpaulin may be used alone as a support for a panel of upholstery on a chair back, if the back is too small or the wood too narrow or delicate to take webbing. And tarpaulin is also used to encase springs incorporated into upholstery.

Fastening Tarpaulin Hessian

12 mm (½ in) improved tacks are generally used for fastening tarpaulin but finer tacks must be used if the wood tends to split easily. As an example of how to fix hessian I

29(a) Tack one side through a folded double thickness ▶

◀ 29(b) Stretch and tack the other sides through a single thickness

29(c) Fold the hessian over and tack it again through a double thickness ▶

Fig. 29 Fastening tarpaulin hessian on a stool

shall take a plain and simple square pin cushion stool (**fig. 29**).

Cut off your hessian a bit larger all round than the size of the seat and then fold over a turning of about 25 mm (1 in) all along one side. Tack this with permanent tacks about 38 mm (1½ in) apart on one side of the stool frame (**a**).

Stretch the hessian tightly and tack along the opposite side through a single thickness, placing tacks about 100 mm (2 in) apart. Repeat this on the other two sides (**b**).

Turn over the hessian and tack through the double thickness, placing the tacks between those underneath (**c**). As with webbing, make sure that the tacks are driven well home with the heads perfectly flat.

In cases where the wood of the chair frame on seat or back is poor or much distressed by previous upholstery tack holes, lines of glue can be laid to assist in holding the hessian, and staples can be used instead of tacks to avoid further damage.

▼ Fig. 30 Tarpaulin hessian as a spring covering

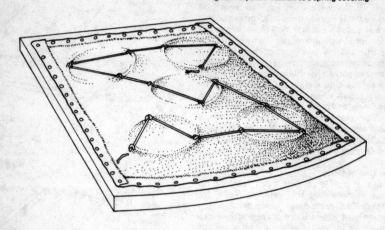

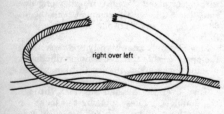

▼ Fig. 31 A reef knot

right over left

left over right

Tarpaulin Hessian as a Spring Covering

A simple chair seat with the springs covered with tarpaulin is shown in **Fig. 30**. You can see that the tacking is done in the same way as on the stool in **fig. 29**, with flanges turned over on the top. A deal of adjustment is necessary to get the springs tensioned evenly, so you should 'temporary tack' through just a single thickness. (In temporary tacking the tacks are driven part way in just so that they hold and can be easily removed.) When all is satisfactory, the tacks can be driven home, the hessian turned back on itself and more tacks placed between the others.

SKILLS WITH CORDS, TWINES AND THREADS

Knots in Upholstery

The diagrams in **figs 31–38** will show you how to tie the knots which are used in upholstery.

The reef knot: this knot is used for joining cords of equal thickness, and the rule is left over right and right over left—pass the left-hand cord over the right-hand cord then the right over the left, repeat and pull to tighten

▼ Fig. 33 Half hitches

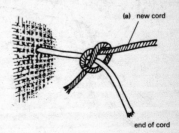

(a) new cord

end of cord

▼ Fig. 32 A sheet bend

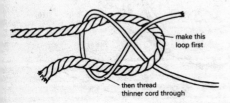

make this loop first

then thread thinner cord through

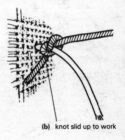

(b) knot slid up to work

(fig. 31). The reef knot is not used very often, but it is useful if you misjudge the length of cord required—say, for lacing springs—and need to join on an extra piece. It can also be used for tying off cottons and twines at the end of a row of stitches.

The sheet bend: this is a knot for joining cords of unequal thicknesses. A loop is formed with the thicker cord and the thinner cord is threaded through the loop, taken round and tucked under **(fig. 32)**; the knot is tightened by pulling on the thinner cord.

Half hitches: the half hitch **(fig. 33)** forms part of several knots and can be used for instance when joining on extra twine for blind stitching or roll-edge stitches, or for joining on another length of thread when ladder stitching, when you need to join the new cord close up to the last stitch made. Make a half hitch by looping your new cord round the old short length. Slide it up to the last stitch that you have made. Then tie another half hitch, looping the new length over the old short end, and pull tight. Do this twice or three times for security, and do not cut off the old end too close to the knots—leave at least 25 mm (1 in).

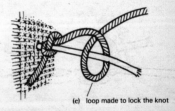

(c) loop made to lock the knot

Fig. 34 The upholsterer's slip knot

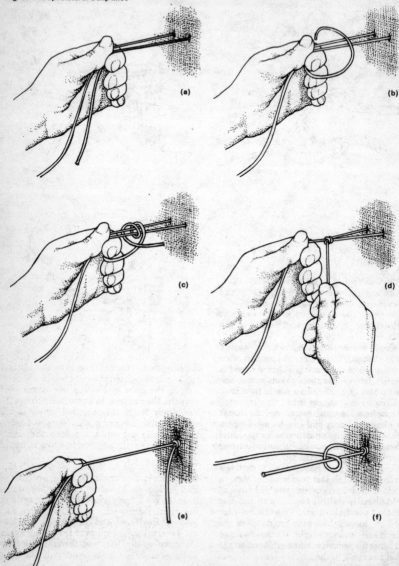

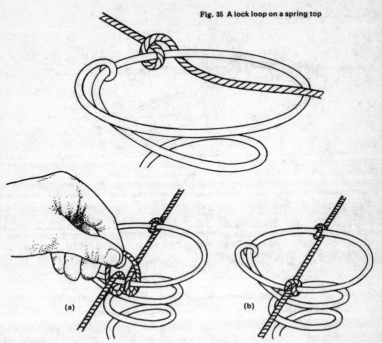

Fig. 35 A lock loop on a spring top

Fig. 36 A clove hitch ▲

The upholsterer's slip knot: this is the knot that is most frequently used by the upholsterer, so you must learn to make it quickly (fig. 34). It is used for fastening twine, thread and cotton to begin a line of stitches or ties and also for tying in stuffings, putting in buttons and for many other jobs. Let us say, for instance, that you are about to fasten a button in some button-back upholstery. There are the two ends of the buttoning twine protruding from the back hessian.

Hold the two ends of twine together between the thumb and forefinger of your left hand (a). The cord end on the right should be at least 100 mm (4 in) behind the finger and thumb. Take the end on the right forward and bend it across the cords in front of your thumb (b). Take the right cord end twice round both cords and through the loop you have made (c).

Pull this cord end to form a moderately tight knot (d).

Pull the other cord to slip the knot up to the required tension, then give the shorter cord a tug to tighten the knot (e).

Lock the knot by looping the longer cord over the shorter one, in three half hitches (f).

The lock loop: this is used when lacing springs with laid cord and as its name implies is not really a knot, but a loop that locks itself and is easily adjustable when loosened (fig. 35).

The clove hitch: to make a clove hitch (fig. 36), which is used on the front part of the coil of a spring, bring the cord over the spring from the back and under, coming up again on the right side of the cord. Hold the cord between the thumb and index finger in a loop (a). Then take the cord over the spring again, this time to the left, and through the loop. Take your finger away and pull the knot tight (b).

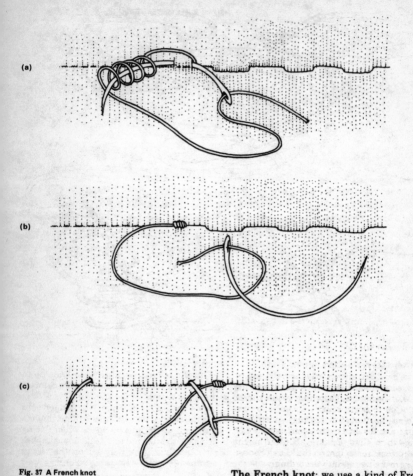

(a)

(b)

(c)

Fig. 37 A French knot

The French knot: we use a kind of French knot (**fig. 37**) for finishing a row of stitches securely.

Make your final stitch very small. Take the trailing thread and wind it round the needle four or five times (**a**).

Pull the needle through and tighten the knot up close to the fabric (**b**).

Make a further two stitches to give length to the end before cutting off so that the knot does not come undone.

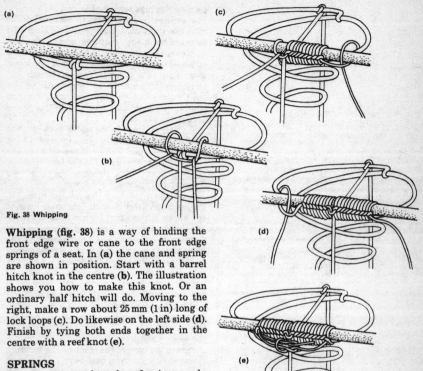

Fig. 38 Whipping

Whipping (fig. 38) is a way of binding the front edge wire or cane to the front edge springs of a seat. In (**a**) the cane and spring are shown in position. Start with a barrel hitch knot in the centre (**b**). The illustration shows you how to make this knot. Or an ordinary half hitch will do. Moving to the right, make a row about 25 mm (1 in) long of lock loops (**c**). Do likewise on the left side (**d**). Finish by tying both ends together in the centre with a reef knot (**e**).

SPRINGS

The size, gauge and number of springs can be varied according to the size and shape of the seat and also to make it harder or softer. Usually springs of 125 to 150 mm (5 to 6 in) will be required, in 10 or 12 gauge. When I am building a new seat I try to keep the person it belongs to in mind, thinking of their height and approximate weight so that I can choose heavier or lighter springs accordingly.

Fastening Springs

In **fig. 39** you can see how to fasten a spring to the webbing support. Use **No. 1** stout twine, as we want the springs to stay there for a very long time. Make three stitches at equal distances round the spring base, fastening each stitch with a half hitch beneath the webbing.

Springs are fastened through the heavy hessian spring covering in the same way.

Fig. 39 Fastening springs ▼

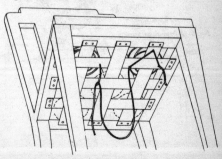

Lacing Springs with Laid Cord

The springs in seats need to be laced down with the stout cord known as 'laid cord'. To measure the length required, stretch the laid cord over the springs from back to front, then add half the length again to allow for knotting. This is a general rule of thumb but obviously it depends on the depth of the built-up edge of the finished seat. For the single chair seat illustrated (**fig. 40**) six pieces of cord are needed.

Tie a single knot in the end of each piece of cord and push a 16 mm ($\frac{5}{8}$ in) improved tack through the knot. Fasten three cords to the back rail and three cords to the left-hand rail opposite the springs. Hammer the tacks into the centre of the wood of each rail.

Hold down the back right-hand spring to the required height—with this chair I would say about 50 mm (2 in) higher than the rails. Tie the cord with a lock loop on the back of the second coil down and a clove hitch on the front of the top coil. This is to keep the spring straighter at the waist; if the cord is tied over the back of the top coil it throws the waist of the spring off-centre and in this position it may buckle after only a short period of use.

Bring the cord forward to the front right-hand spring. Tie a lock loop on the back of the top coil then a clove hitch on the front of the second coil down.

Fasten the cord to the front rail by twisting it round a tack driven half-way in. When you have adjusted the tension correctly drive the tack home and tie a half hitch round the cord to make it secure.

Take the end of the cord back up to the top coil of the front spring. Pull the cord fairly tight, then tie it off with a clove hitch and a half hitch.

Repeat this procedure with the other cords and your seat should end up looking something like the seat in **fig. 40**. Note the position of the laced springs and how they are 'fanned' out. Test each spring by pressing it down; it should go down in an arc to a perfectly upright position when compressed. Notice how the 'knuckles' of the springs are facing inwards and the knuckles on the bases of the springs are positioned on webbing and not over a space between the webs. It is very important for the long life of springs to position them correctly.

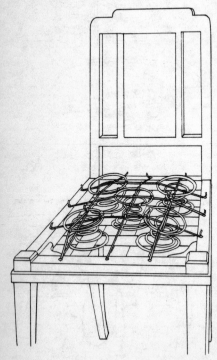

Fig. 40 Lacing springs with laid cord

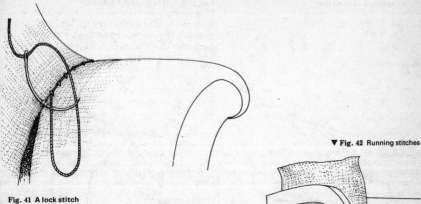

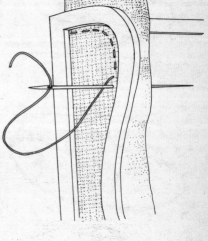

▼ **Fig. 42** Running stitches

Fig. 41 A lock stitch

HAND SEWING

Sewing with Twine

The lock stitch shown in **fig. 41** is useful when
it is necessary to seam hessians, say at the
junction of the hessian first stuffing covering
of an arm and the back of an easy chair. This
stitch is really a series of knots along the
seam. Use a fine **No. 3** or **No. 4** twine with a
large curved needle. Make a straight stitch
joining the two pieces of fabric. Then, holding the twine tightly in the direction of stitching, catch up the edges of the two hessians.
Bring the point of the needle out beneath the
taut twine so that in fact it is passing through
a loop and as you pull the stitch up it forms a
half hitch knot.

There are easier stitches that you make
with twine. A simple running stitch is used
for fastening two layers of hessian (**fig. 42**).

The 'locking back stitch' is similar to the
blind edge stitches which I will deal with at
the end of this chapter (pages 47–49) and is
used when joining the first stuffing covering
of scrim hessian to the basic support hessian
where stitched edges are to be formed. In **fig.
43** you see it being used on the back of an
iron-frame crinoline chair.

▼ **Fig. 43** A locking back stitch

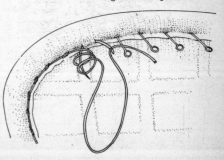

Fig. 44 Ladder or slip stitching

(a)

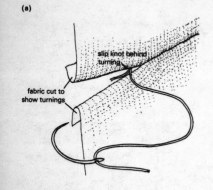

slip knot behind
turning

fabric cut to
show turnings

(b)

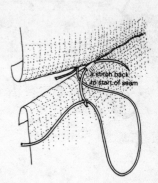

a stitch back
to start of seam

(c)

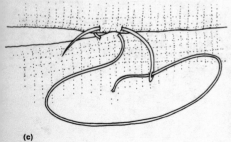

Sewing with Thread and Cotton

The ladder or slip stitch: modern upholsterers
often fasten outside seams with small gimp
pins or with 'back tacking strip', a metal
band with protruding spikes. But, to my mind,
on a quality piece of upholstered furniture
all outside seams that cannot be machine
stitched should be hand stitched with small,
neat, ladder stitches. The method is illustrated in **fig. 44**. For most jobs a 75 mm (3 in)
17 gauge curved needle is the most suitable.

To begin, take a small stitch just beneath
the overlapping covering material, 10 mm
($\frac{3}{8}$ in) to the right of the beginning of the
seam (**a**). Secure the stitch with an upholsterer's slip knot.

Take a stitch through the line of the fold
of the overlapping cloth back to the beginning of the seam (**b**). This makes a secure
start to the sewing and also obscures the
knot and thread end, which can now be
tucked away beneath the fold.

Take the first stitch in the direction of
sewing by making the point of your needle
enter the opposite fabric a thread or two back
from the place where the last stitch emerged
(**c**). You can now see the reason for the

(d)

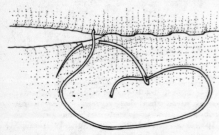

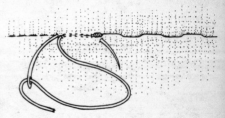

(e)

curved needle, for the two pieces of cloth that are to be sewn together are stretched taut, and nearly always there is a part of the wooden frame beneath. Sewing with a straight needle would prove extremely difficult.

The rule that the next stitch should be started a thread or two back from where the needle last emerged applies all the way, so that as you pull the thread tight after each stitch, it disappears completely (**d**). The length of stitch is determined by your cloth. For heavy, coarsely woven fabrics, such as tweed, a stitch of up to 15 mm ($\frac{5}{8}$ in) is acceptable. But for finer fabrics, a 5 to 10 mm ($\frac{3}{16}$ to $\frac{3}{8}$ in) stitch is much neater.

When you come to the end of the seam, the thread must be securely finished off, so use the French knot described earlier. Do not cut off the thread at the knot, or it will soon come undone. With the needle still threaded, take two or three stitches back along the seam (**e**), then cut the thread off close to the surface of the cloth. Alternatively, if your seam ends at the bottom of the chair, you can put in a tack underneath, wind the thread round it and then drive the tack home to hold the thread.

Fig. 45 Sewing on braid

Fig. 46 Sewing on fringe

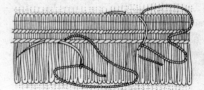

Fig. 47 Sewing on decorative chair cord

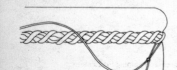

47(a) ▲

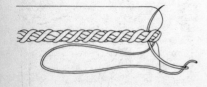

47(b)

Sewing on Braid and Fringe

It is a good idea to fasten braid with adhesive first, and I shall deal with this later in this chapter in the section on using adhesives (pages 50–51). But you must not rely upon adhesive alone for fastening, because after a year or two it very often deteriorates and, at the slightest provocation, your trimming will be hanging off making everything look very tatty. Always sew braid as well, for that extra security.

Stitch the braid as shown in **fig. 45**, catching the top loops of the braid to the fabric underneath. If possible, put another row of stitches along the bottom. Use a matching cotton and make the stitches very small so that they cannot be seen.

I do not use adhesive for fastening fringe but fix it with two rows of stitches, as shown in **fig. 46**. The top stitches are exactly the same as for braid, but the second row consists of simple in-and-out stitches which hold in the lower part of the fringe.

Sewing on Decorative Chair Cord

It is nice to know how to fix decorative chair cord, for as a trimming this always sets off a chair well and gives it a more luxurious look. Chair cord is a silken twisted cord, usually about 6 to 10 mm ($\frac{1}{4}$ to $\frac{3}{8}$ in) in diameter. You can choose cord either to match or to contrast with the colour of your chair covering.

When you intend to trim with this cord, simply ladder stitch the seams in the places where it is to be used—usually the arm scrolls, front border, wings and maybe the top of the outside back. After this, pin the cord in position over the seams and sew on with a fine 75 mm (3 in) 19 gauge curved cording needle (**fig. 47**).

47(c) 47(d)

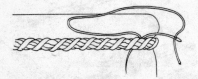

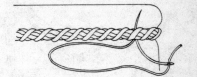

Begin with a small stitch and a slip knot which will be concealed beneath the cord (**a**).

Make a stitch sideways through the centre of the cord (**b**).

Going back from this a fraction, make the next stitch about 10 mm (⅜ in) beneath the cord and in line with the ladder stitches (**c**). When it emerges bring the needle to the opposite side of the cord.

Backing again a fraction from the end of the last stitch, make a further stitch at 90 degrees through the centre of the cord (**d**).

Continue in this fashion along the length of the cord. Be particularly careful to fasten the cord securely at the end. And before cutting your cord do wrap it round with a piece of transparent adhesive tape and then cut through the centre of this. If you do not do this the cord will fray out and untwist in no time.

Incorporating Piping into a Seam

Lastly, in this hand-sewing section, let me show you how to sew piping into a seam. For an example I will describe how to fit a facing to an arm front scroll.

First, fix the piping with pins beneath the lip of the scroll's edge.

Next, pad out the facing with suitable stuffing (hair and wadding). Cut the material roughly to shape and fix it on, using the same pins removed one at a time and put back, this time also catching the folded-in edge of the covering.

Finally, sew in the facing cover and the piping together, using a sort of ladder stitch but going through the flange of the piping at the line of machined stitches each time you make a stitch in the facing or the inside of the scroll lip (**fig. 48**).

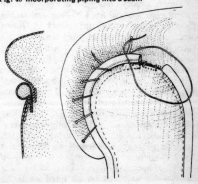

Fig. 48 Incorporating piping into a seam

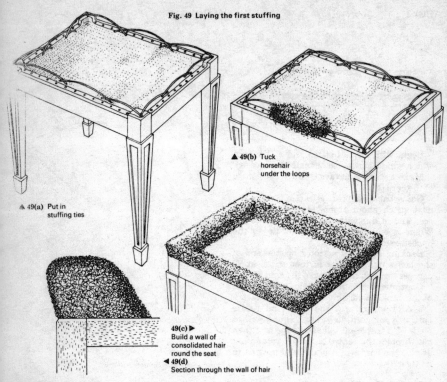

Fig. 49 Laying the first stuffing

▲ 49(a) Put in stuffing ties

▲ 49(b) Tuck horsehair under the loops

49(c) ▶ Build a wall of consolidated hair round the seat

◀ 49(d) Section through the wall of hair

THE TRADITIONAL STITCHED ROLL EDGE

Very occasionally I have had in my workshop ancient chairs on which I have found traces of some of the original upholstery. A Queen Anne period chair had an edge made of rolls of straw bound with twine. An early Georgian chair had gained a little in sophistication, with horsehair instead of straw and the edges sewn rather in the way mattress borders used to be stitched. Then I have found chairs from the late eighteenth century into the late nineteenth century with much improved upholstery foundations and stitched edges to everything, elaborate scrolls on arms and back panels as well as to seat fronts, all done in the way I shall now show you. It is a way of achieving firm upholstery that will retain a shape yet will not be so hard as to be uncomfortable. As an example I will take an ordinary stuffed-over stool seat.

The First Stuffing

When the basic support of webbing and hessian has been put on, the next step is to lay a first stuffing of horsehair (**fig. 49**).

Using your largest 100 or 125 mm (4 or 5 in) curved needle, put in stuffing ties (bridle ties) of **No. 3** twine 25 mm (1 in) from the edge (**a**). Notice the back stitch between the loops.

Tuck well carded horsehair, a small handful at a time, under the loops of twine (**b**), to form a wall of fairly consolidated hair all the way round the seat (**c**). In the enlarged inset (**d**) you will see the shape to aim for. Corners are difficult, but try to get them as firm as the rest of the edge. You can do this by rolling in extra hair, which will bind on to the hair

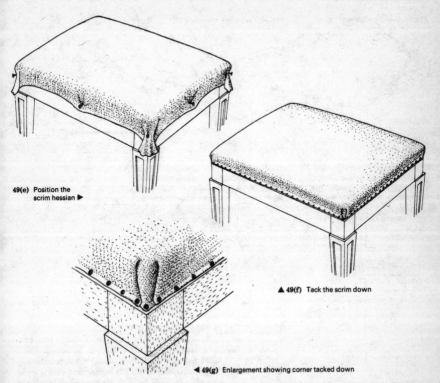

49(e) Position the scrim hessian ▶

▲ **49(f)** Tack the scrim down

◀ **49(g)** Enlargement showing corner tacked down

already held by the ties. Do a real bit of sculpting to get these edges as close to the shape that you want for the finished job; this means straight, even, slightly overhanging the frame and pretty firm. Fill up the centre now, aiming at a slightly domed shape with the middle about 38 mm (1½ in) higher than the edges.

Now for the hessian. I think scrim hessian is best for this work, although 280 g (10 oz) will do. Measure and cut off a piece, allowing an extra 25 mm (1 in) all round to turn in. Mark the centre of each side of your stool and the centres of the four sides of your piece of hessian. Lay the hessian over the stuffing and position temporary tacks at the marks. Next, temporarily tack the corners, just one tack in each, pulling the scrim fairly tight to give a little tension (e). Now fasten all round

the stool with temporary tacks. Be careful to keep the threads of the weave of the scrim running parallel to the edge of the frame.

You will have noticed the chamfer along the edge of the seat rail; it is on this that the scrim is permanently tacked. Drive in the tacks at intervals of about 20 mm (¾ in) carefully aligning the tacks along a thread of the scrim. Your edges will then be the same height all the way round (f). Fasten the corners last. The inset (g) shows the best way to do it. Tack the centre of the corner, then make a small pleat on each side. You will have to make many adjustments to the corners before you get them right; try to get them to the same height and overhang as the rest of the edge and with the same density of stuffing, even if you have to ram a little more hair in before finally tacking down the scrim.

Fig. 50 Using a regulator

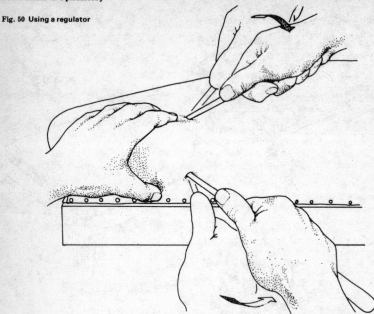

Fig. 51 Putting in through stuffing ties

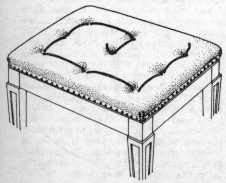

Using a Regulator

At this stage of your upholstery you can practise 'regulating'. It looks so simple but I find many folk do not grasp what regulating is all about. With a little practice you should be able to redistribute stuffing that is within the confines of scrim hessian to any shape desired. Of course, you will not have to do this to any great extent as you will already, so cleverly, have got most of the hair in an even and orderly shape. But should there be a hollow or a lump that has missed your dexterous fingers this can now be rectified with the regulator. In the drawing (**fig. 50**) you can see how to use this. Simply push the regulator into the stuffing to about a third of its length and, keeping the fulcrum at the place where the regulator enters the hessian, lever the horsehair filling into the hollow or away from the over-full area, as you will.

Through Stuffing Ties

Through stuffing ties (**fig. 51**) are used to anchor the top scrim hessian through the stuffing to the hessian and webbing underneath. With a crayon or felt tip pen and an upholstery gauge (page 11), mark the top hessian in the form of a rectangle with the sides 100 mm (4 in) from the seat edges. Take a 250 mm (10 in) double-pointed needle and thread it with **No. 1** stout twine. In one corner of the marked rectangle make a stitch about 15 mm ($\frac{5}{8}$ in) long, taking it through the seat. Tie the stitch off loosely with an upholsterer's slip knot. Proceed as you see in the drawing, finishing up with one stitch in the very centre of the seat. Pull down the ties tightly, holding the slack as you do so with each tie in turn, starting with the first slip knot and ending with the centre stitch. Fasten off this centre stitch with a number of half hitches. Unthread the needle and put it safely away. Nasty accidents can happen with these double-pointed needles—especially when they are left somewhere with twine dangling. If the twine gets caught round a leg or a foot it may pull the sharp needle into a position to inflict a painful wound. I speak from bitter experience.

EDGE-STITCHING

Now you are ready to try your skill at a stitched edge. I shall tell you *how* to do it first, then at the end it will be clearer and more easy to explain *why* we do it. Thread your 250 mm (10 in) double-pointed needle with about 3 m (10 ft) of **No. 3** twine. When edge-stitching work from left to right, or the other way round if you're left handed. On this stool we are going to put in two 'blind' rows and one row of 'through' stitches to form a roll edge.

Describing this method of stitching in words is difficult, but I will do my best to make it clear with the help of the drawings (**fig. 52**).

Face one side of your stool and start by pushing in your needle on the line of tacks 30 mm (about 1$\frac{1}{4}$ in) from the left-hand corner. The point should come through the top about 90 mm (3$\frac{1}{2}$ in) back from the edge (**a**).

Pull the needle through just as far as the eye. Give the needle a bit of a twist in an anti-clockwise direction to 'scoop' horsehair inside the seat with the eye-end point of the needle (**b**).

Push the needle back so that it emerges at the far end of the corner, again just on the

Fig. 52 Edge stitching

(a)

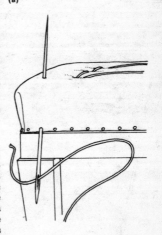

(b)

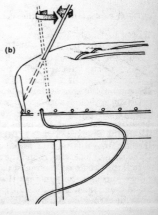

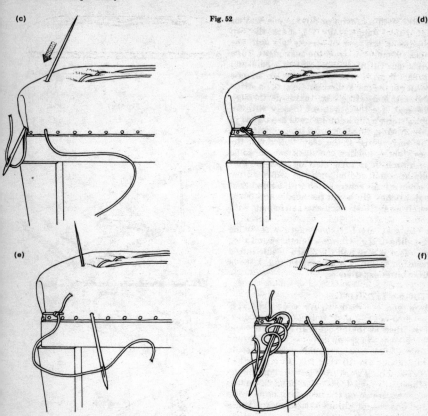

(c)

Fig. 52

(d)

(e)

(f)

line of tacks (the point of the needle should actually scrape the wood of the frame) (**c**).

Pull the twine through, tie it with an upholsterer's slip knot and pull it tight (**d**).

Push the needle in again 38 mm (1½ in) to the right of the knot at the angle shown (**e**).

Do the anti-clockwise 'scoop twist' as in (**b**) then return the needle so that about half its length comes out at the front at the point where the first stitch ended. Take the twine leading from this starting stitch and wind it three times, clockwise, round the needle (**f**).

Pull the needle right out and the twine will follow through the windings that you have made round the needle. Pull the whole length of twine through and tighten the stitch.

Carry on stitching in this manner round your stool until you come back to your starting place, then tie off the end of twine to the short end of the starting stitch (**g**). It often happens that you run out of twine before you reach the end of a row. If so, join on more twine with half hitches. By the way, do dress the twine with beeswax—it will be less likely to kink and knot up when you are stitching. Use your regulator now to work up the hair and even out the edge and then put in another row of blind stitches in the same way, this time 12 mm (½ in) above the first row.

Now we have to put a roll round the seat edge to give it crispness and definition when it is covered. The method is similar to the blind stitching, but it differs in that the stitches go through to the top. Use your regulator once again to bring up the edge and really consolidate the hair inside. Feel with your fingers to see that there are no soft or lumpy places along this edge. If there are, deal with them with the regulator. Now, with your upholstery gauge and felt tip pen mark a line about 23 mm ($\frac{7}{8}$ in) in from the edge on the top (**h**). Draw another line round the sides 23 mm ($\frac{7}{8}$ in) down—or just above the second row of stitches.

With a rectangular seat it is best to put in a single stitch in each corner—just single through loops of twine about 20 mm ($\frac{3}{4}$ in) long tied with a slip knot and fastened off with a couple of half hitches (**i**). These give a good tension along the edges.

Begin again on one side of your stool, 20 mm ($\frac{3}{4}$ in) from a left-hand corner, pushing your needle through the marked line on the front and coming through the line drawn along the top. Take the needle right out, then push it back through as near to the left-hand corner as possible. Guide it so that it comes out on the front line. Tie an upholsterer's slip knot and pull the twine up tightly. For the next stitch, push the needle 25 mm (1 in) to the right of the first stitch. Guide the needle so that it comes through the hessian on the line you have drawn along the top. Now pull the needle right through and pass it back through the edge at the place where the first stitch finished. Wind the twine around the needle three times, just as you did with the blind stitches (**j**), and pull it up very tightly in the direction of stitching, using the fingers of your left hand to squeeze the stitch together as you pull. Carry on round the seat and when you reach your starting place again tie the twine to your first stitch with a reef knot. A section through the edge, illustrating a firm, round roll formed in the manner described is shown in (**k**).

So now you see what we are trying to achieve with edge stitching. With the blind stitches we are gradually bringing forward and binding the horsehair into a dense wall at the edge. We then top this with a neat roll. And here we have an edge strong enough to be sat on and remain in shape and yet not so hard as to cause discomfort to anyone who sits on the stool.

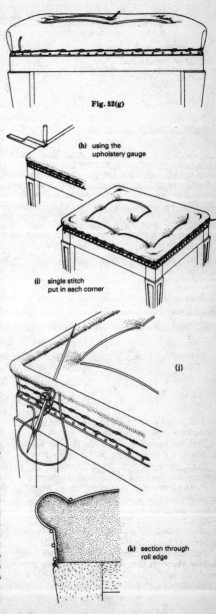

Fig. 52(g)

(h) using the upholstery gauge

(i) single stitch put in each corner

(j)

(k) section through roll edge

Fig. 53 Fastening braid with adhesive

53(a) Secure the end of the
braid with gimp pins

53(b) Apply adhesive to the fabric

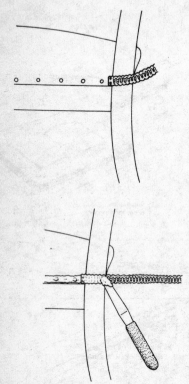

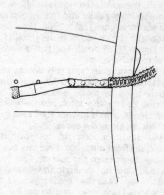

53(c) Spread adhesive along the braid

USING ADHESIVES IN UPHOLSTERY

There are several uses for adhesives in upholstery. Very often a standard-sized rubber
cushion made of foam will require pieces
added to make it up to the desired size or
shape. For building on there is a special
impact adhesive with a 'soft bond', which
means that you do not end up with a hard line
of glue along the join. There are a number of
adhesives for fastening braid as a trimming.
One of these is a latex preparation which has
to be used with great care, for if any is spilt
or splashed on the covering it is practically
impossible to remove it without making a
mark. The adhesive that I favour is a thixotropic impact adhesive. Because it is a jelly,
it is easy to dispense and does not come off
the spreading knife in long, unmanageable
strands, which is what happens with most
impact glues. Also, because it only sticks
tightly when firm pressure is applied, if you
stick the braid lightly at first you will be able

53(d) Press the braid into position
with your fingers

53(e) Fold the end under

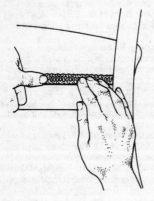

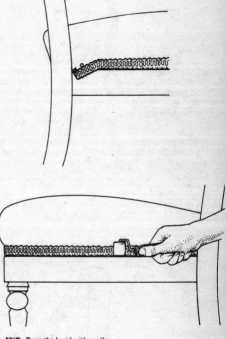

to remove it to readjust if necessary. The
following instructions apply to both of these
adhesives (**fig. 53**).

Secure the end of the braid to the chair fabric
with two gimp pins (**a**).

Apply a line of adhesive to the fabric (**b**).
Spread the adhesive along the braid, holding
the braid taut and scraping the glue along to
ensure a thin, even application (**c**). Do not
lay the braid down to spread the adhesive—if
you do this the adhesive may go through to
the face, especially with a thin braid. Coat no
more than 50 cm (20 in) of braid at a time.

Stretch the braid along the fabric, gently
pressing it down with the fingers (**d**).

To finish off, cut the braid 6 mm (¼ in) too
long and fold this extra under. Put another
dab of adhesive on the folded piece and press
it back into position (**e**).

Leave the adhesive to set for a few minutes,
then roll the braid with a small seam roller
(**f**) and stitch it as described on page 42.

53(f) Press the braid with a roller

MODERN UPHOLSTERY

I do not intend to say a lot here about modern upholstery, except to mention a few hints regarding maintenance and replacements, and to tell you how a modern piece of furniture can be reupholstered in a traditional way. Some other aspects of modern upholstery are covered in Chapter 6 where I show you how to reupholster a wing fireside chair.

Replacing Rubber Webbing

Rubber webbing, which is used a great deal in modern upholstery, needs to be replaced after a few years. The better chairs have webbing straps with metal fixing clips which fit into slots in the seat rails. You can make up new pieces by buying rubber webbing and the end clips.

Before cutting off the lengths of webbing, you must allow for stretching to give a bit of tension. With webbing of average thickness, straps up to 30 cm (1 ft) long should be 25 mm (1 in) shorter than the distance between slots; straps over 60 cm (2 ft) should be shorter by 12 mm ($\frac{1}{2}$ in) for every 30 cm (1 ft). Make the straps a little longer than this if the webbing is particularly thick, a little shorter if it is very thin. The end clips must be very securely clamped on to the webbing. They should be squeezed in an engineer's metal working vice, then hammered down on a piece of thick iron plate so that the metal clip really grips the rubber. Narrow rubber webbing, such as is sometimes used in chair backs, can be fixed with large-headed tacks or by two lines of 10 mm ($\frac{3}{8}$ in) staples, driven in with a staple gun.

Transforming a Modern Chair

I must tell you about Brenda's chair because this shows how it is possible to take an unattractive piece of modern furniture and transform it into something good.

Brenda came for her second year to our class with a tale of woe: she had now reupholstered nearly everything in her flat and had nothing left to do; in her desperation she brought along a small, modern television or sewing chair, just a seat and back job, there it is in the picture (fig. 54). Well, she spent an evening stripping it down to the frame and then we got our heads together. Someone said, 'What about a buttoned back?' Then

Fig. 54 A small modern sewing or television chair

54(a) Before

54(b) After

there was a suggestion from someone else about putting in a conventional coil spring seat instead of the unit that it had had before. 'A double-bordered seat?' said Brenda, with a glint in her eye. Then I remembered a pair of cabriole legs that had been lying about in my workshop for at least twenty years—when we tried them they were just the size. So off came the nasty, thin, splayed front legs, and on with the 'Queen Anne's'. These made a stronger job of the frame too, as they had square posts at the top which fitted inside the frame. These legs were well polished by Brenda, who was by now getting very enthusiastic. You can see in the illustration

what a transformation she worked on this chair. The back has side scrolls built up with proper stitched edges. And the seat also is built up, with multiple rows of blind stitches and a roll edge. This proved to be a good practice piece for traditional upholstery methods. Covered in a strong, small-patterned cotton print and trimmed with a silken cord it has become a very desirable, expensive-looking sewing chair. I suppose that the lesson to be learnt here is, that we should not look with disdain on all modern furniture when it has reached its life's end, but should try to see what possibilities there are for transformation.

4   The Drop-In Seat

The drop-in seat is an entirely separate removable seat frame upholstered and fitted within the seat rails of a chair or stool. These seats, sometimes known as 'trapseats', are found in dining chairs, footstools, and larger stools such as dressing table and piano stools. This is the ideal task for the beginner. It is something that I like the students in the class that I teach to have for their first job, because it gives a gentle introduction to some of the basic skills of upholstery.

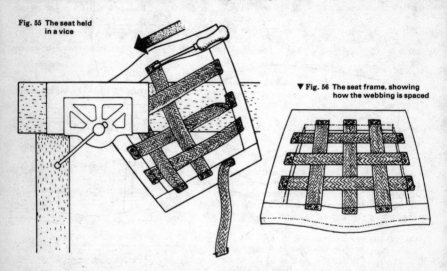

Fig. 55 The seat held in a vice

▼ Fig. 56 The seat frame, showing how the webbing is spaced

Measuring

And so to begin; measure the seat while the old covering and upholstery are still on. With your flexible steel measure take a reading over the seat from back to front. Allow plenty under the seat for turning, for you will be turning in and neatening off the material when you finally tack it down. Many loose seats are finished with a covering of hessian or lining over the underside; I always view these with suspicion and get the feeling that the upholsterer had something to hide. You, on the other hand, are going to be proud of your upholstery and leave to view the facts of good workmanship and best quality materials.

Ripping Off

For directions on ripping off, refer to Chapter 3 (page 28). Stripping a small item like this chair seat will be much easier if you can use a carpenter's vice to hold it as you work (fig. 55).

When the frame is bare, examine the joints to make sure they are sound and well glued. It can be very frustrating to get all the new webbing stretched on tightly only to find that the joints are giving way and the whole frame is in danger of coming apart. Test the joints by tapping inside the frame with a mallet to see if they will come apart, or try twisting the frame, for this will also show any give in the joints. There is one more test to do before proceeding further and that is to place the seat frame in the stool or chair to check on the fit. If you are using a thicker covering cloth you may have to plane off some wood to allow for this, or if the cover was originally poorly fitted you may have to glue on thin strips of wood to make up the gaps.

Webbing

Having just read the chapter on basic skills, you will be familiar with the methods of fixing and stretching webbing (pages 29–30). 'Yes, but how many pieces of webbing should I put on?' you ask. Well, webs should be no more than 50 mm (2 in) or the width of the webbing apart (fig. 56). An average-sized single chair seat takes three pieces from back to front and two or three pieces from side to side. A large carver chair may perhaps need four strips back to front and three across. Over the webbing is stretched 450 g (16 oz) tarpaulin hessian (fig. 57). For directions on fastening I refer you again to Chapter 3 (pages 31–32).

The Stuffing

To anchor the stuffing in place, stuffing ties in the form of large stitches (page 44) must be put into the hessian in lines across the seat (fig. 58a). These ties should be fairly taut.

For the best and most lasting results use a good quality horsehair stuffing. Tuck lines of stuffing under the ties, as in fig. 58b. If these lines of hair are placed evenly and are of uniform density and size, the even distribution of stuffing over the seat will be assured. The next step is to fill in between these lines of hair. Then tease over a further layer of hair to form a dome-shaped mass, as in fig. 58c.

The amount of stuffing required will depend upon the quality of the horsehair, as the shorter hair consolidates under hard pressure, while the better quality long, curled horsehair will stay risen and springy until confined by the undercovering. If you are doing a set of chairs it is a good idea to weigh out equal amounts of stuffing to get all the seats to the same size and shape.

The Undercovering

The next stage is to pull the mass of horsehair down to the desired shape by putting

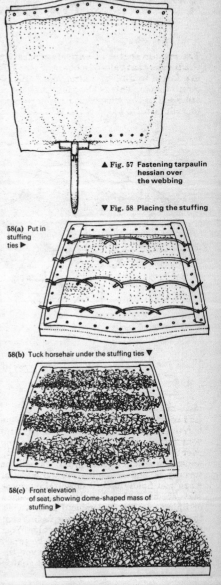

▲ Fig. 57 Fastening tarpaulin hessian over the webbing

▼ Fig. 58 Placing the stuffing

58(a) Put in stuffing ties ▶

58(b) Tuck horsehair under the stuffing ties ▼

58(c) Front elevation of seat, showing dome-shaped mass of stuffing ▶

Fig. 59 Putting on an undercovering

▲ 59(a) Position the undercovering over the stuffing

◀ 59(b) Place temporary tacks in the centre of each side

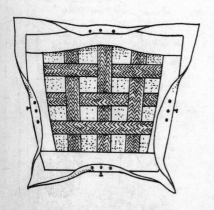

▲ 59(c) Temporarily tack the undercovering to the underside of the seat rails

on an undercover. Some upholsterers, for reasons of economy and speed, use no undercoverings at all, but with you speed is not so important as quality of workmanship; and, when you consider the high cost of the covering material, it is as well to employ methods that will prolong the life of the fabric. And that is just what an undercover will do—as all the strain of containing the filling and securing the basic shape is taken by a simple, strong but cheap woven fabric. I use a good unbleached calico for undercoverings. Roughly measure the size required and tear off the fabric. Make a small snip and then rip across; the calico will tear along a thread and your piece will be nice and square.

Fig. 59 shows you how to put on the undercover. At **(a)** we see the calico lying loosely over the hair, having been positioned so that there is an equal amount of material hanging down each side. Drive in four temporary tacks—12 mm ($\frac{1}{2}$ in) fine tacks—just far enough to hold, in the centre of each side **(b)**. Turn and hold the seat with its back edge on

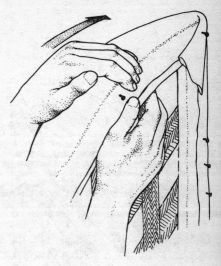

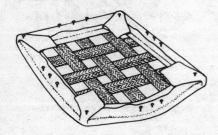

▼ **59(d)** Temporarily tack the corners

59(e) Stretch and smooth the undercovering ⬍

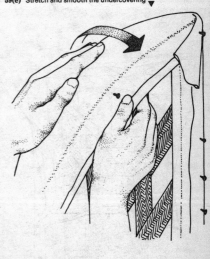

the bench and, (if you are right-handed), the left edge towards you. Put three temporary tacks in the centre of the underside of each rail (**c**). Then remove the first temporary tacks. This temporary tacking is very important, allowing you to adjust and position the covering before permanently fixing it. Gently stretch the calico at the corners, pulling diagonally and placing temporary tacks as shown in (**d**). The diagonal stretching at each corner gives tension along all four sides and you can see that it immediately gives the whole seat an even, domed appearance. Keep a constant eye upon the line of threads in the centre of the calico, so that they remain straight from back to front and from side to side. Any deviation indicates that you are stretching too far on one side or the other.

Still holding the seat on its edge, take out the three temporary tacks in the centre of the front edge. Tuck back any hair that has worked over the edge of the wood. Stretch the cloth as in (**e**). If you are right-handed, pull the cloth with your right hand, using your

59(f) Temporarily tack again ▼

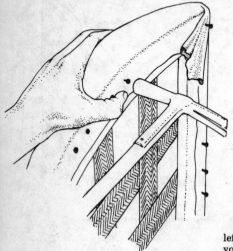

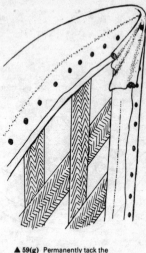

▲ 59(g) Permanently tack the corners

59(h) Pleat the corners ▶

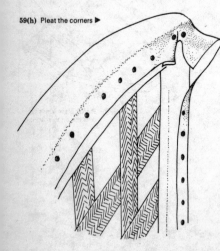

left to smooth and compress the stuffing. As you adjust the cloth, put in temporary tacks again. Stretch the cover and place a tack in the centre and then, work away from yourself, by smoothing and stretching the fabric with your left hand along the front of the seat. This action takes up any fullness and eliminates 'tack marks'—lines which run from the tack, making a small groove over the seat. These will appear if the fabric is pulled very tightly at the point where it is held by the tack while remaining looser between tacks. A couple of strokes, then smooth and stretch from back to front, with your right hand still holding the edge of the cloth. Do not pull—merely anchor the material and take up any slack brought over by the smoothing and stretching.

On the last stroke of your left hand, bring your thumb over and use it to hold the cloth while the right hand picks up the tack and hammer to secure it temporarily (f). Repeat this procedure on the other three sides of the seat to a point 70 mm ($2\frac{3}{4}$ in) from the corners.

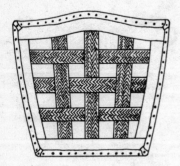

◀ 59(i) Permanently fix the undercovering

Pull down the corners again (**g**), and this time drive a tack right home in the position shown.

Continue the stretching process right up to the corners, pleating in the corners neatly as in (**h**). Now permanently tack with 10 mm ($\frac{3}{8}$ in) fine tacks all round the seat as in (**i**), keeping within 12 mm ($\frac{1}{2}$ in) of the outside edge. Remove the temporary tacks and trim off surplus calico.

Your seat should now have assumed a good, even, fairly firm shape. But note how the horsehair is working through the weave of the cloth. Hair will work through almost any cloth except the hairproof ticking used for mattresses. So we must arrest its progress with something that it cannot penetrate—cotton wool, cotton felt or wadding.

Cut off two layers of wadding for extra security and lay it on top of the undercover. Trim the wadding around the edges as in (**j**), so that none will extend over the sides—remember that the seat has to fit into the chair frame.

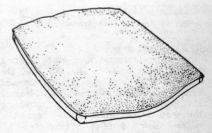

▲ 59(j) Place cotton wadding over the undercovering

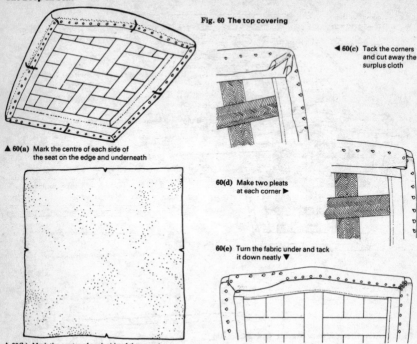

Fig. 60 The top covering

▲ 60(a) Mark the centre of each side of the seat on the edge and underneath

▲ 60(b) Mark the centre of each side of the covering material with a small V

◄ 60(c) Tack the corners and cut away the surplus cloth

60(d) Make two pleats at each corner ►

60(e) Turn the fabric under and tack it down neatly ▼

The Top Covering

Now we come to the final stage—putting on the furnishing fabric (**fig. 60**). Mark the centre of each side of the seat on the edge and underneath with a soft pencil (**a**). Measure the length and width of the seat, measuring the width at the front, where the seat is widest. Allow a turning of 38 mm (1½ in) all round. Refer to Chapter 3 (pages 27–28) for directions on cutting the fabric. When you have cut the piece of cloth to size find the centre of each side by folding the cloth in half, first lengthways and then widthways, and nicking the corner of the fold so that a small V is made in the exact centre (**b**).

Lay the cloth over the seat and adjust the position until you are satisfied that the marks on the frame correspond with the V cut in the cloth. If, because of the shape of your seat, the marks on the sides do not meet when the cloth is adjusted properly, make sure that they are the same distance apart on each side. Temporarily tack, just as you did with the undercover, but this time you must take even more care to keep the weave straight back to front and side to side.

The corners must be neatly pleated. Permanently fix a tack in each corner, then cut away the surplus material in the form of a square up to the tack (**c**). You can see at (**d**) how the two pleats on one of the corners are made. These can be permanently fixed as shown. Finally, turn the material under and tack it down neatly all round (**e**).

POST-WAR LOOSE SEATS

Many of the cheaper dining chairs made in the 1950–60s had no webbing in the seats but just a piece of plywood or even hardboard nailed on the frame. The stuffing was either made of cotton wool felt or polyether (polyurethane) foam. This early foam was very

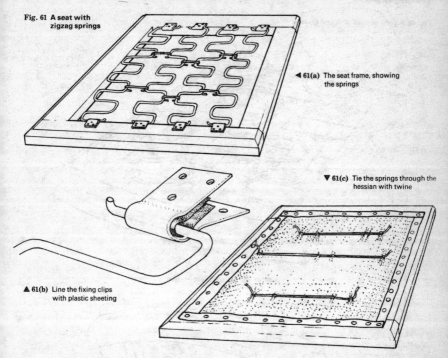

Fig. 61 A seat with zigzag springs

◄ 61(a) The seat frame, showing the springs

▼ 61(c) Tie the springs through the hessian with twine

▲ 61(b) Line the fixing clips with plastic sheeting

unstable and after a year or two would disintegrate into a powder or sticky granules (the modern equivalent, however, is very long-lasting). If the frame of this type of seat is robust, you can remove the plywood board and reupholster it with webbing as described in Chapter 3 (pages 29–31), but if the seat frame relies upon the plyboard for strength, and you want a comfortable seat then perhaps you should consider making up new stouter frames.

SEATS WITH ZIGZAG SPRINGS

Many modern seats have springs of the zigzag strip kind, sometimes called ripple wire springs (fig. 61a). Very little can go wrong with these springs so long as they remain linked together laterally. Wire links or small tension springs are used for this purpose. However, these do sometimes get noisy after a year or two and squeak when the chair

is sat on. So, when reupholstering, remove the springs and line the fixing clips with a material such as a thick leathercloth or plastic sheeting (b).

These seats are very simple to upholster. Just cover the zigzag springs with stout tarpaulin hessian stretched over fairly tightly and tacked in the usual manner—the springs should be tied through at several points along their length (c). On top of the hessian place a layer of thick cotton felt and secure it with a few through ties of twine. Then add a layer of 25 mm (1 in) thick polyether foam to make a very comfortable seat.

To cut the foam, lay the seat on top of the foam sheet and cut round it with a very sharp knife, keeping about 10 mm ($\frac{3}{8}$ in) outside the frame. With some shears or scissors, chamfer the top edges of the foam and then cover it with a calico undercover as described on pages 56–59.

The Drop-In Seat

Fig. 62 A drop-in seat with coil springs

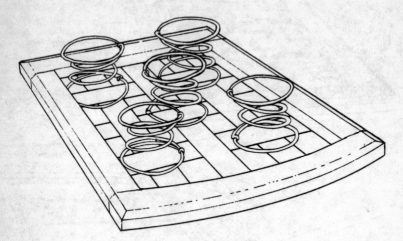

▲ 62(a) The five springs in position

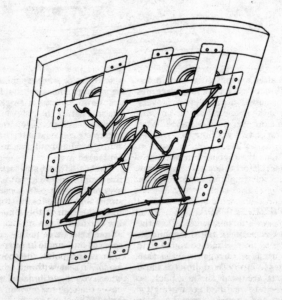

62(b) Fasten the springs to the webbing

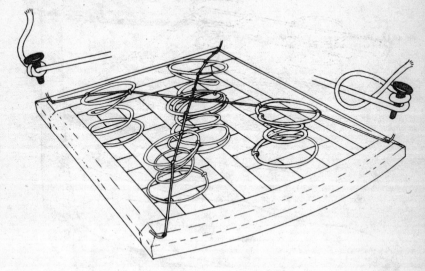

62(c)   Lace the springs with two diagonal ties

DROP-IN SEATS WITH COIL SPRINGS

Some good class dining chairs made before the Second World War had small coil springs in the loose seats (fig. 62). The springs are usually four or five in number, about 75 to 100 mm (4 to 5 in) high and gauge 12. When working on a chair of this type, you can either dispense with the springs and re-upholster it as just described, or re-make it as a spring seat. The springs will need renewing. Place the webbing under the frame and tie the springs to the webbing at the usual three points on each spring base (page 37). If there are five springs, place the first in the centre and fasten it. Then sew on the other springs mid-way between the frame and the centre spring to form a square round it (a) and (b). If only four springs are used these are placed in the form of a square but closer together in the centre of the seat. Pull the springs down well with laid cord using two diagonal ties (c). Again, I refer you to

Chapter 3, pages 37–38, but note that the cord is knotted on the top coils of all the outside springs with these seats and not on the second coil down as previously described. Because the springs are very short there will be little or no distortion at the centre waist of the springs. When you have finished lacing, the centre spring should be no more than 75 mm (3 in) high.

Stretch 450 g (16 oz) tarpaulin hessian over the springs and tack it down in the same way as you did with your loose seat. Then, with stout twine, stitch the tops of the springs to the hessian in the same way as you fixed the bottoms of the springs—so that they are attached at three points round the top coil, secured by a single knot on each stitch (c).

From this point, the procedure is the same as for a seat without springs, except that when you have finished you will need to cover the underside with hessian or lining to hide the webbing and make a neat finish.

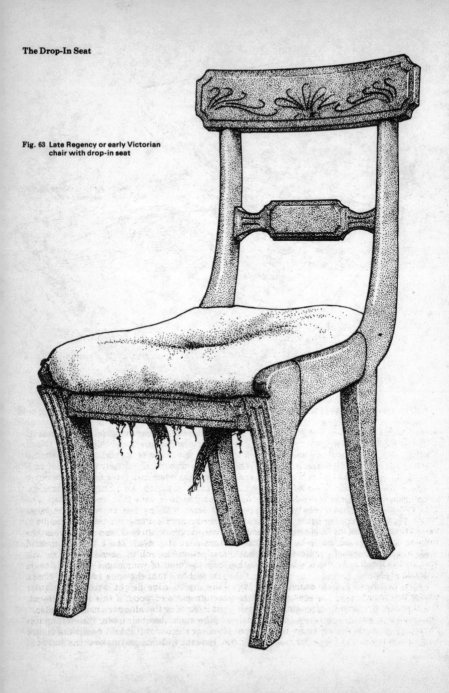

Fig. 63 Late Regency or early Victorian
chair with drop-in seat

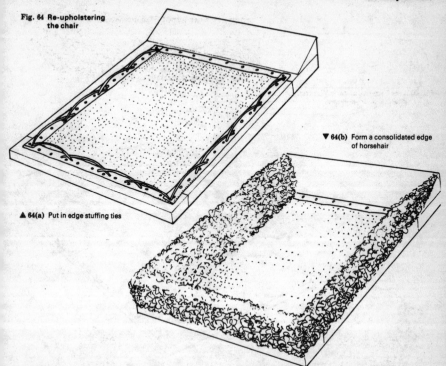

Fig. 64 Re-upholstering the chair

▲ 64(a) Put in edge stuffing ties

▼ 64(b) Form a consolidated edge of horsehair

REGENCY AND EARLY VICTORIAN LOOSE SEATS

There is one more form of loose seat that I would like to mention—the type found on dining chairs of the Regency, William IV and early Victorian periods. The seats fit between raised side rails and are prevented from slipping forward on the chair seat frame by a peg which protrudes from the centre of the front rail of the chair and fits into a corresponding hole in the frame of the loose seat. These seats are a little more complicated to uphol-ster, as the front and sides are built up with stitched edges.

Let us examine a typical example (**fig. 63**), one which looks as if the seat is about to fall through. The black shiny material with which it is covered—probably the original covering—is made of horsehair interwoven with cotton or linen and is called hair seating.

This is a very strong, durable material and is, I believe, still made to this day.

The job is quite straightforward at the start—you can call on your previous experi-ence to take you to the stage where you cover the new webbing with tarpaulin hessian. Once you have done that, the next step is to put some stuffing ties in with your large circular needle along the two sides and the front, approximately 20 mm ($\frac{3}{4}$ in) from the front edge (**fig. 64a**). These ties are to hold and retain the roll of horsehair which will form the core of your edges. On some seats you will find that the back has already been built up to edge height with a triangular section piece of wood; if this is not present, put in stuffing ties along the back edge also.

Now tuck horsehair under the stuffing ties to form a dense roll (**b**). Then fill the centre of the seat with hair to just over the height of

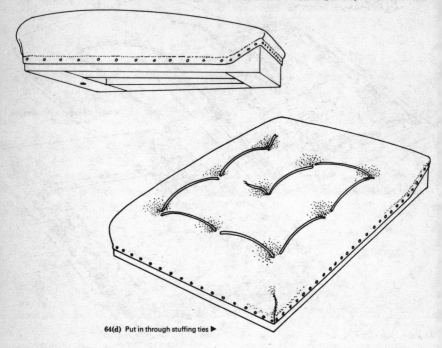

▼ **64(c)** Fasten the first stuffing covering

64(d) Put in through stuffing ties ▶

the edges. Tack on the first stuffing covering of scrim hessian (**c**). Hold on, you say, what height does this edge and seat need to be? If you place the loose frame in the chair seat, the raised side rails will give a good indication of the thickness of the seat needed because the finished height should be just above these rails. And if there is a wooden raised edge at the back of the seat frame, this will also show the intended height.

The method of covering the first stuffing is as follows. Measure and cut off a piece of scrim hessian large enough to cover the seat. Mark the centres of each side of the seat frame and the centres of the four sides of the hessian and temporarily tack the hessian, matching the marks just as you did when covering the other loose seat. There is usually a small chamfer along the top edges of the frame—if there is not, it is a good idea to

make one with a plane or rasp—and it is along this chamfer that the line of permanent tacks is placed. Use 10 mm ($\frac{3}{8}$ in) tacks and place them about 20 mm ($\frac{3}{4}$ in) apart. Start in the centre of the back and when you are tacking the front and the back follow a thread of the hessian with the row of tacks. Slight adjustments must be made at the corners, a thread or two being taken up here. Do not try to follow a thread when tacking along the sides—the seat is narrower at the back. The front edge should overhang the frame by about 15 mm ($\frac{5}{8}$ in) (**c**). The sides should also overhang, but to a smaller degree. Remember, the seat must fit between the side rails of the chair. Use your regulator at this stage to adjust the stuffing beneath the hessian and manipulate the corners into sharp, square shapes.

When your first stuffing is adjusted and

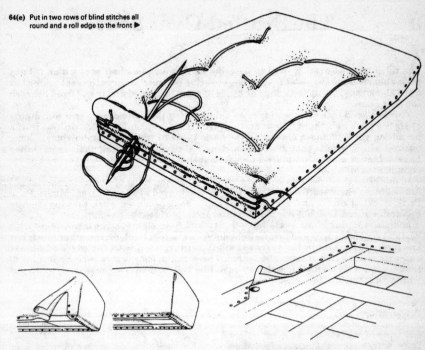

64(e) Put in two rows of blind stitches all round and a roll edge to the front ▶

▲ **64(f)** Pleat the material neatly at the corners

▲ **64(g)** Cut away the fabric to leave the peg hole uncovered

regulated so that all the edges are straight and true, put in the through stuffing ties (**d**), this time going right through the seat and anchoring the scrim hessian to the webbing and hessian beneath. Using an upholstery gauge and a felt tip pen, mark a rectangle 100 mm (4 in) from the seat edges. Put in your through ties with stout **No. 1** twine, starting at a back corner and finishing in the centre (pages 46–47).

Follow the procedure for edge stitching outlined in Chapter 3 (pages 47–49) putting in two rows of blind stitches all round but making a rolled edge to the front only (**e**).

On a seat like this, roll edges are not needed on the sides as the side edges are protected within the confines of the chair rails. If you have a carpenter's vice you can use it to hold the chair seat while you work. But this aid is not essential.

Put on the top stuffing, undercover, wadding and covering fabric in exactly the same way as you did on the dining chair seat—with the exception of the corner pleats, which on this seat must be single. At (**f**), you can see exactly how they are made. The material is pulled diagonally towards the corner and fixed at the front with two tacks. The surplus material is then cut away up to the tacks and the pleat is folded neatly and squarely up to the corner. With some materials, the pleat may be sewn up to make an even neater job, using the ladder stitch described on pages 40–41.

There is one final point. When you are neatly turning in and finishing off the material under the seat, do not forget to leave the hole for the peg uncovered. At (**g**), you can see how to cut the fabric in a V up to the hole.

5   The Stuffed-Over Seat

The term 'stuffed-over' is used to describe an upholstered chair seat which is built permanently on to the chair frame. The covering is stretched over the seat and either fixed along the sides up to facings or beads of wood or turned under and fixed beneath the seat rails.

This is a good task for a beginner as upholstering the stuffed-over seat of a dining chair is a job small enough to undertake even if work space is limited or time is at a premium; yet it includes almost all the basic tasks of traditional upholstery. I have noticed with students that after completing a stuffed-over dining chair seat, if they have achieved a good standard of craftsmanship, they begin to sail through more complicated jobs.

In our class there are two students who have, during most of one term, specialized in the dining chair stuffed-over seat and have achieved near perfection. Michael and Paul, working slowly and very painstakingly, have produced work that looks quite professional and each has put his own interpretation into the shaping.

Michael's dining chair seats have a classical, late eighteenth century look with vertical stitched edges and just a slight dome to the top. Paul, on the other hand, has interpreted his seats in the early twentieth century way, with the edges shallower and extending well out from the frame. These examples show that there is a lot of scope, even with a small upholstery task like this stuffed-over seat, for you to put your own stamp on the work.

Preparation

There is such variety among the shapes, sizes and types of stuffed-over seats, but we shall begin with a simple, straight-edged dining chair seat like the Regency chair in **fig. 65**. The seat of this chair looks quite hollow— it has reached a stage where it might collapse and fall through at any moment. Take off the old upholstery in the usual way with the ripping chisel and mallet (page 28). If you find it difficult to remove the tacks, and especially if it is a rather precious chair, use pliers and pincers. There are no springs in this seat, so the webbing goes on top of the rails. You know all about webbing (pages 29–31), but as this chair has a fairly wide seat I would advise putting four pieces of webbing each way. Fasten tarpaulin hessian over the webbing.

Stuffing and Covering

Now we come to the first stuffing. No doubt, you will have removed the old first stuffing with the stitched edges still intact, and, you say, 'Couldn't we just put this back?'. Edges which have remained in good shape can be

saved and put on again, provided they are well vacuum cleaned, then covered with hessian and stitched again. But I would rather you made up a new edge for your chair. Seeing a job right through is the only way to learn.

Put in the stuffing ties about 25 mm (1 in) from the edge of the frame all the way round (**fig. 66**). Then tuck and shape the horsehair under these ties to make a wall of stuffing on all four sides. I would advise you to make this wall about 10 mm ($\frac{3}{8}$ in) higher than you intend the edge to finish, and to extend it out so that it overhangs the rails by about 20 mm ($\frac{3}{4}$ in); however, this is a matter for your own interpretation. Fill up the centre of the seat with hair to form a domed shape (pages 44 and 55).

To cover this first stuffing you can use scrim or 280 g (10 oz) hessian. I like to use scrim as it is stronger and more manageable. Measure and cut off a piece, allowing 25 mm (1 in) all round for turnings. Mark the centres of the front and back of the scrim and also the centres of the front and back rails of the chair. Lay the scrim over the stuffing and

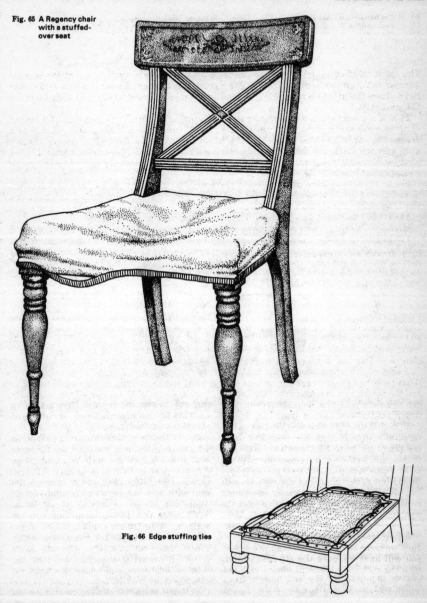

Fig. 65 A Regency chair with a stuffed-over seat

Fig. 66 Edge stuffing ties

Fig. 67 The hessian cut away from the back upright ▼

Fig. 68 The surplus to be cut off at the corners ▼

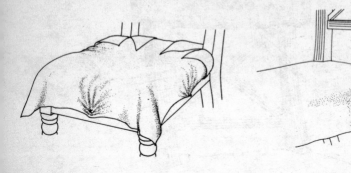

Fig. 69 Through stuffing ties placed ▶

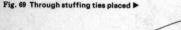

position it at the front and back marks with temporary tacks.

After making sure that the threads of the scrim are straight, lay back the two back corners as shown in **fig. 67** and cut from the corner of the scrim to within 10 mm (⅜ in) of the back upright. Turn over the scrim, cut off the surplus and, using the regulator, tuck in the remainder (**fig. 68**). Put in temporary tacks all the way round the seat, adjusting until you are satisfied with the shape. Then turn in the scrim and fasten it permanently along the tacking chamfer on the edge of the frame, placing the tacks no more than 20 mm (¾ in) apart. Work to the weave when fixing the back and front so as to keep the edges uniform in height and the back and the front of the seat parallel. Because of the domed

shape of the seat top you will have to take up a thread or two near the back uprights and also at the front corners.

Put in through stuffing ties to pull down the centre of the seat and hold the filling in place (**fig. 69**). Now stitch the edge, following the procedure laid down in Chapter 3 (pages 47–49). Two blind rows are needed on the two sides and the front; one blind row of stitches is usually sufficient at the back. When you come to put in the through stitches to form the roll edge, begin with the front edge—and do not forget the single stitch at the right-hand corner. After you have stitched the front, continue on the right side as far as the back upright, then stitch the left side, doing the back last.

Next, put in lines of stuffing ties for the top

Fig. 70 Placing the top stuffing ▼

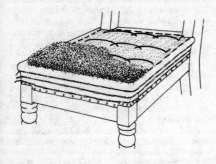

Fig. 71 Cardboard stiffener fitted at a corner ▼

▼ Fig. 72 An undercovering of calico

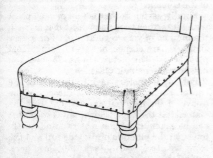

▼ Fig. 73 Surplus fabric to be cut away from the back upright

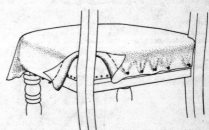

stuffing and pack stuffing under them. In **fig. 70** notice how the filling 'feathers' off at the roll of the edge. It is very important that no hair is left hanging over the rolled edge.

To keep the front corners in good shape and to give support to the covering material and in particular to the corner pleats, it is as well to cut and fit some stiffeners (from medium thickness cardboard) and tack them around the corners as shown in **fig. 71**.

The next step is to fasten on an under-covering of calico, to pull down and contain the top stuffing, bringing the seat to its finished shape (pages 55–57). The calico should be fixed to the sides of the rails, with no turnings (**fig. 72**). Put one or two layers of cotton wadding over the top of the under-covering, to prevent the hair penetrating and

also to insulate the two covers and give a little extra richness to the feel of the seat.

Now, there are one or two points to note when you come to put on the top cover. Firstly, when you have marked the centres of the back and front of the cloth, positioned it and temporarily fastened it with three or four tacks on each side, cut the two corners into the back uprights as you did with the scrim covering, up to within 6 mm ($\frac{1}{4}$ in) of the wood (**fig. 73**). Take care when you are cutting off surplus material, lay the material in to see just how much you can cut away, then tuck and turn it in to the back uprights. Stretch these turnings down and temporarily tack them.

The second point relates to the front corners. In my opinion these always look best

The Stuffed-Over Seat

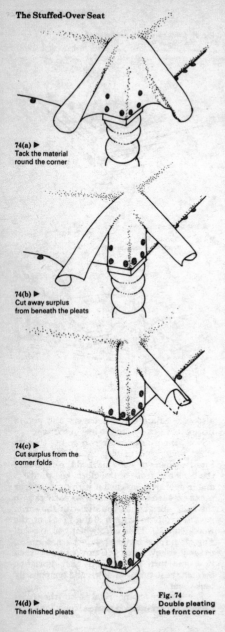

74(a) ▶
Tack the material round the corner

74(b) ▶
Cut away surplus from beneath the pleats

74(c) ▶
Cut surplus from the corner folds

74(d) ▶
The finished pleats

Fig. 74
Double pleating the front corner

when they are double pleated (except where the corner has been made sharp and square). The drawings in **fig. 74** show you how this is done. Stretch and tack the corner of the material in the centre of the seat corner, positioning the covering so that there is equal fullness on each side of the centre of the corner. Tighten and tack the material round the corner, but making sure the tacks are far enough away from the corner to be obscured by the pleats (**a**). Cut away surplus material up to these tacks to eliminate bulk beneath the pleats (**b**).

Fold in the pleats and, holding each one down with the point of your regulator, note where the double fold comes at the bottom; cut off any remaining surplus material there is here, so as to keep the material as close and flat as possible—you do not want any lumpiness that would ruin the evenness of the line of the trimming (**c**).

Finally, fasten down the fold of each pleat with tacks, then tuck and press the folds with the flat end of your regulator (**d**). For a very sharp, square corner, however, a single-fold pleat is best. The pictures in **fig. 75** show you how to make a single pleat.

Put one temporary tack to the side of the corner, making sure that the threads of the weave of the material are vertical. Cut the material at the angle shown in (**a**) so that it can be taken under the seat rail and neatly folded at the junction of the side rail and the front leg. Temporarily tack the fabric here. Cut off the surplus material (**b**).

Fold the fabric under, bring it round the leg corner and fasten it with two tacks on the front of the leg top, placing the tacks at least 20 mm ($\frac{3}{4}$ in) in from the corner so that they will be obscured by the pleat (**c**). Cut off surplus material, as shown in (**d**).

Fold in the pleat so that its edge comes right up to the corner. Hold this down with the point of your regulator and cut off the surplus material from the double thickness at the bottom of the pleat, and also cut up to the junction of the front rail and the leg (**e**).

Lastly, fasten the pleat with two tacks, as shown in (**f**). For extra neatness, these single pleats may be sewn up with very small ladder stitches. Begin sewing from the top of the pleat, making sure that you hide the starting knot inside the fold.

Fig. 75 A single-fold pleat for a sharp, square corner

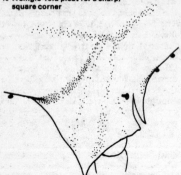

▲ 75(a) Cut the material at the angle shown

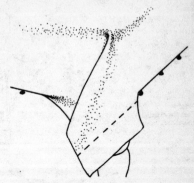

▲ 75(b) Cut off the surplus material

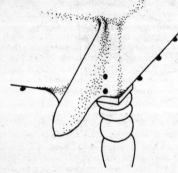

▲ 75(c) Tack beneath the pleat

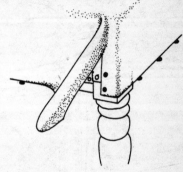

▲ 75(d) Cut off the surplus

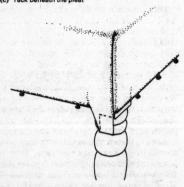

▲ 75(e) Cut the surplus from under the pleat

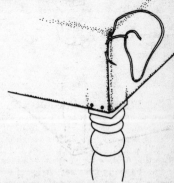

▲ 75(f) Fasten the pleat with two tacks

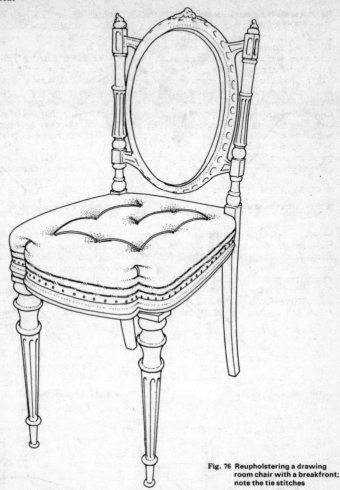

Fig. 76 Reupholstering a drawing
room chair with a breakfront;
note the tie stitches

A SEAT WITH A BREAK FRONT

An attractive drawing room chair with a
break front, i.e. the line of the front of the
seat is broken near the corner, is shown in
fig. 76. I would like to point out the difficulties that arise when you come to re-make
an edge shaped in this way. A lot of upholsterers will ignore the shape of the frame and
upholster the seat as though it just had a D-
shaped front, but where possible the roll edge
should always follow the line and shape of
the frame. Constant regulating at the internal
corners when putting in the rows of blind
stitches will keep the edges of this break
front seat well defined. Then, before starting
the through roll stitches, put in a single tie
stitch, as shown in **fig. 76**, to pull the angle in
sharply. Roll stitch in the usual way.

SINGLE CHAIR SEATS WITH SPRINGS

If you have a single chair with springs I would refer you back to Chapter 3, pages 37–38 for directions but an extra point to note here is that the tarpaulin hessian used to cover the springs should not be pulled any tighter than the spring lacings, or these will just hang loose and serve no purpose. The springs are sewn to the hessian with the usual three stitches per spring and the procedure is the same as for a chair with no springs—with one exception. When you put in the through stuffing ties, these should only go in as far as the spring hessian and not right through the webbing.

A SEAT WITH A SERPENTINE FRONT

The reupholstery of a seat with a serpentine or double-curved front requires particular care. When you are putting on the scrim hessian much adjustment and temporary tacking will be needed to achieve a good shape that follows the line of the frame. Start as usual, tacking from the front centre, and as you proceed outwards from here, take up and almost gather the scrim towards the centre (fig. 77). There should be no tension across the protruding centre curve. If you

tighten the scrim as you work outwards you will eventually lose this curve, as it will be forced back.

COVERING SHAPED SEATS

When you come to the job of covering seats that have elaborate shapes such as break fronts, serpentine and pronounced D fronts, it is possible to cover them in just one piece of material; when you do so, many temporary adjustments have to be made to eliminate most of the fullness around the fronts and sides. But although you eventually achieve a good appearance, it is later, after the chairs have been in use, that wrinkles and looseness form around the upright borders of the seat, as the upholstery is compressed.

To avoid this problem, cover the seat top separately first, sewing this cover all round just beneath the lip of the roll edge. Then make a separate border by sewing a strip round the seat. The join between the two can be trimmed with chair cord (fig. 78). If the border is padded out just a little this makes a really first class job and everything will be smooth, there will be no fullness or gathering and, of course, no corner pleating to bother about.

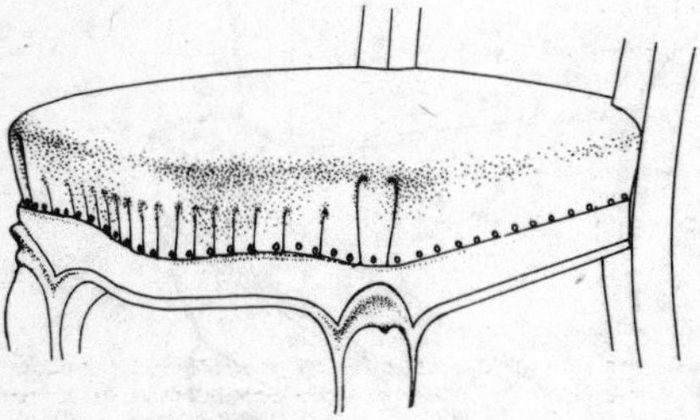

◀ Fig. 77 A seat with a serpentine front, showing gathers made in the scrim in the front

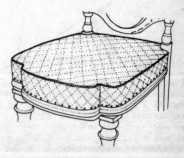

Fig. 78 A shaped seat bordered and trimmed with chair cord ▶

6   A Modern Wing Fireside Chair

To show the techniques of modern upholstery I have chosen to reupholster a wing fireside chair. So that I can cover most of the methods that have been used in the trade in recent years I have included design points from many leading makes (fig. 79), so please do not take this model and expect to find that the chair you are working on has exactly the same construction and innovations. When measuring up this chair use the chart, fig. 25 in Chapter 3, showing each cut. This is a project of medium difficulty.

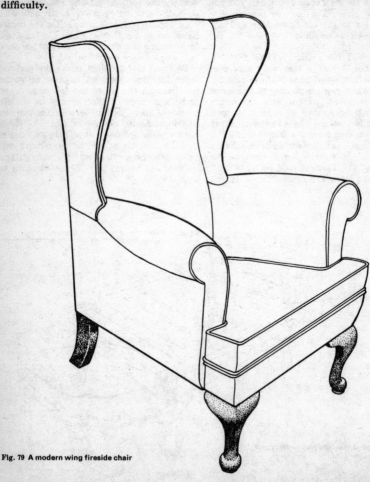

Fig. 79 A modern wing fireside chair

Removing Staples

Staples used with staple guns are a very quick and efficient way of fastening modern upholstery, but they take a lot longer to remove than tacks. You can try using a ripping chisel, but unless the wood is very soft all you will do is cut off the tops of the staples, leaving sharp little needles of steel which are difficult to extract. I find that the best way is to prise the staples up a little by pushing a regulator point underneath. This makes them sufficiently proud for your pincers or adapted side-cutting pliers to be used.

Stripping the Chair

Turn the chair upside down and unfasten the material round the bottom of the frame. Then you can remove all the outside coverings. You will see that the wings, which are made of solid wood, are screwed with three or four screws to the back upright. Unscrew and remove the wings. The bottom of the wing boards are usually held by one or two dry

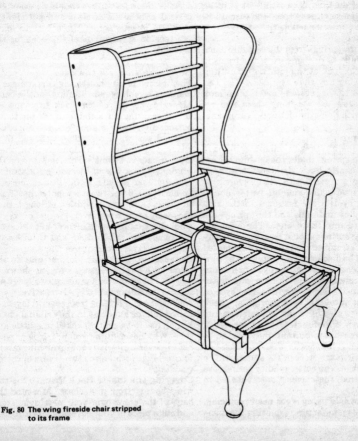

Fig. 80 The wing fireside chair stripped to its frame

dowels, so lift the wings upwards to remove them. Take note of the upholstery and the way in which it has been done as you strip the chair, especially if the covering is the original. Remove all the cotton felt filling from the wings and discard this, it has become too hard and consolidated, and soiled where heads have rested for many years. The same applies to the cotton felt stuffing on the arms, but I think that you can leave the rubberized horsehair pads that are underneath; having been kept from the light, these are as good as new.

The inside back upholstery is of kapok and this has deteriorated into lumps and fine particles of dust, so take it off—it is made up in a separate closed case—and discard it. The cushion interior has perished, so throw this away too.

Remove the springs from the seat and place them carefully to one side. Now the frame is bare (**fig. 80**), look at the joints, dismantling and re-glueing any that are loose. You can then attend to the legs and make them look like new again by stripping them and re-polishing with French polish or polyurethane.

Tension Springs

The best quality fireside chairs still have coil tension springs under the cushions. Less expensive chairs have the tension springs fastened to the rails with clips, eyelets or hardened steel nails and on better chairs webs with eyelets are fastened to the side rails with glue and nails and the springs are then hooked into the eyelets. The most important seat springs should be examined. Any that have stretched and have coils pulled apart must be discarded and replaced by new ones. The tension springs that you find under the back upholstery are thinner and softer and are usually fastened with screw eyes or staples put into the back uprights; check these springs also for wear or looseness and replace them if in doubt. Getting springs of the right length is important; they need to be about 25 mm (1 in) shorter than the distance between fixings; no more or the spring will be over-stretched. The better quality springs are fabric covered, the cheaper ones encased in plastic.

When the side fixing webs need replacing, write to the manufacturers quoting the name and number of your chair and they will usually send a renewal pack complete with instructions. However, certain chairs with side webs will present a puzzle for you because the webs seem to be fastened so that the fixing nails are obscured by the bottom tacking rail of the arm. How on earth do we get these webs off, let alone fix the new ones? Well, if you look at the outside of the arm you will see that the tacking rail is fastened to the back upright with one screw. Remove this screw and you will be able to take the rail out, because the front end is only held by a dry dowel. Now you can get at the webbing.

If there are other methods of holding the springs, these fastenings should be examined carefully for signs of wear and put right if they are unsatisfactory. It is best to leave the tension springs out of the seat for the moment.

New Upholstery for the Back

The first job in reupholstering this chair is to make up a replacement stuffing for the back. Measure the size of the back from the extremities of the sides and from the top to the bottom and, using a good strong calico, cut out and sew up a case that is 50 mm (2 in) wider and 25 mm (1 in) longer than these measurements. I think we can improve on the original kapok filling by making a stuffing of foam and acrylic wool. Cut a piece of 12 mm ($\frac{1}{2}$ in) flame-resistant polyether foam to 25 mm (1 in) less in width and length than the inside back; wrap several layers of acrylic wool sheeting round this core. Put the stuffing inside the calico case, and if necessary add more layers to improve the shape. Sew the case up. Tack this stuffing unit to the frame with a roll-over at the top, as shown in **fig. 81**. Put in through stuffing ties (page 46) to hold the filling in place. Alternatively, you can make a good filling from several layers of cotton felt, or kapok as in the original chair. Kapok has to be gently packed in a little at a time. Whichever filling you use, it is as well, before covering it with your furnishing fabric, to overlay it with one or two layers of cotton wadding.

Covering the Inside Back Remove the two wing boards from the chair. Measure the back of the chair over your new upholstery and cut a piece of your covering fabric to fit.

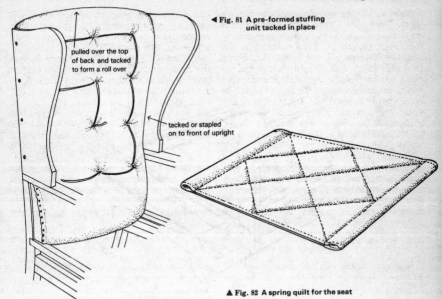

◀ Fig. 81 A pre-formed stuffing unit tacked in place

pulled over the top of back and tacked to form a roll over

tacked or stapled on to front of upright

▲ Fig. 82 A spring quilt for the seat

The tension of the fabric on this type of chair back is critical. It must not be stretched too tightly or you will just be pushing the soft tension springs in; and it must not be loose, or after some use the covering will develop wrinkles or fullness. Take particular care with the diagonal corner tension, so that when you stretch the fabric to the corners you get rid of all the edge fullness and no pleats or gathers are necessary anywhere. I have seen some of these chairs upholstered by people with perhaps only a little experience, who have put pleats in or gathered up the material when, if only they had spent another ten minutes or so in further temporary tacking and adjusting, they would have found that every part could be smooth and shapely. Take this as a rule for every part of this chair; no unsightly fullness anywhere in the covering.

Making a Spring Quilt for the Seat
If the seat springs are left exposed, the cushion cover tends to suffer and when you turn the cushion over you find that the springs have left their impression in the form

of indented lines which take a long time to disappear. A spring quilt (**fig. 82**) laid over the springs will prevent this sort of damage.

Put back the tension springs so that you can take a couple of measurements. It is a good idea to start by making a drawing of the shape of the seat. Then measure and note the width across the seat at the front spring between the spring fixing webs and the width at the position of the back spring.

Now, measure the length from the back to the front springs and mark it on the drawing. Transfer these measurements to a piece of fairly stout black platform cloth or lining or even a good quality calico, adding 12 mm ($\frac{1}{2}$ in) to each side for seaming and 75 mm (3 in) to the front and the back for the pockets for the springs. Cut two pieces to this size and shape. Cut a piece of 12 mm ($\frac{1}{2}$ in) flame-resistant polyether foam to the exact size of your drawing. Put the two pieces of platform cloth together and seam down each side on your sewing machine. The lines of stitches should be 10 mm ($\frac{3}{8}$ in) in from the edges. Turn this open-ended bag the right side out, and lay the piece of foam inside, equidistant

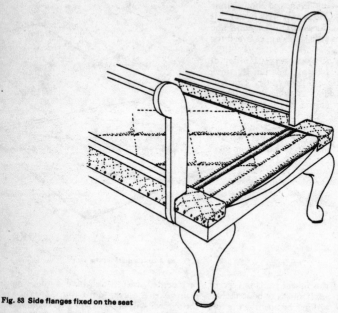

Fig. 83 Side flanges fixed on the seat

from the ends. Sew a row of stitches 20 mm ($\frac{3}{4}$ in) in from each side to hold the foam in place, then lay the quilt over the springs. To gauge the exact length which is to be hemmed, mark on the cloth where the back and front springs come. Fold over a wide hem at the back and the front, allowing at least 30 mm ($1\frac{1}{4}$ in) from the edge to the stitches to make a pocket large enough for the spring to go through. Stitch along these hems, finishing off neatly with returned stitches. Now draw some very light diagonal pencil lines across the quilt to form a series of diamond shapes. Follow these lines with stitches and there you have a very professional-looking quilt. Remove the back and front springs and thread them through the hem pockets of the quilt, then hook the springs back on again. The spring that lies exactly between the two arm front uprights has to be left above the quilt because this will hold the back of the small seat platform.

Making Side Flanges for the Seat
Also to protect the cushion from wear from the springs, make two side flanges that will overlap the quilt (fig. 83). These can be made and fastened as you see in the illustration. Each piece is hemmed on three sides then fixed on the top of the seat rail and on the front rail. Notice how the flanges dip under the tension spring reserved for the platform and border fastening.

The Front Seat Border and Seat Platform
Next, cut out and stitch up a covering for the small seat platform and front border (fig. 84). There are two ways of making a covering. If the material is plain, you can cut out the covering in one piece, (a) so that it extends from behind the tension spring that is above the spring quilt to 50 mm (2 in) under the front seat rail. Lay the piece of material over this area to be covered and pin the corners to form a box shape. Remove the piece of

material and stitch the two pinned-up corners on the sewing machine and then cut away the surplus cloth leaving flanges of about 13 mm (½ in). A patterned cloth may look better if it is made up in two pieces with a top panel and a border; you can pipe the seam between the two (**b**).

Whichever method you use, sew a flap or fly piece such as lining, hessian or thick calico to the back of the cover. The free long edge of this flap is then taken underneath the tension spring that is on the top of the quilt, brought forward and tacked on to the front seat rail as you can see in (**c**). This flap now forms a floor for the platform and border padding which can be made from foam or two layers of cotton felt. Draw the cover down over the padding and temporarily fasten it beneath the front rail, cutting the cloth in at the legs. The final fastening can be left until all the covering has been done.

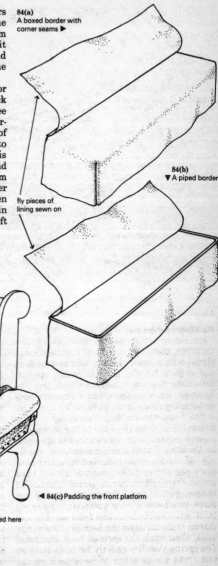

84(a)
A boxed border with corner seams ▶

84(b)
▼ A piped border

fly pieces of lining sewn on

cover thrown back

◀ 84(c) Padding the front platform

fly tacked here

Fig. 84 The front seat border and seat platform

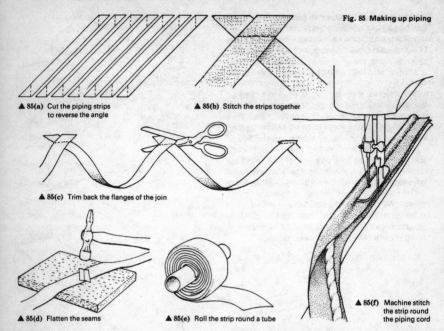

Fig. 85 Making up piping

▲ 85(a) Cut the piping strips to reverse the angle

▲ 85(b) Stitch the strips together

▲ 85(c) Trim back the flanges of the join

▲ 85(d) Flatten the seams

▲ 85(e) Roll the strip round a tube

▲ 85(f) Machine stitch the strip round the piping cord

Making up Piping

I mentioned piping above, and I think this would be the moment to make up sufficient for the whole chair—for the border (if piped), the scroll fronts to the arms, round the outside of the back and wings, and, of course, the cushion (fig. 85). So measure round everything to see how much you need.

Take your furnishing fabric and, using tailor's chalk, mark out the strips for the piping diagonally, at an angle of roughly 45° to the weave. Piping strips should always be cut on the bias, from the bottom left to the top right of the fabric, to give a good even shape to the piping when it is stitched. This is because in most fabrics the more robust threads run across the width, and these put up more resistance against the drag under the foot of the sewing machine. The strips should be at least 60 cm (2 ft) long. For No. 1 piping cord they need to be 38 mm (1½ in) wide. Thicker or thinner cords need correspondingly wider or narrower strips to give the required flange to the piping.

When you have cut the required number of strips, join them to make one long length. The joins must show as little as possible, so this is what you do. The end of each strip is at an oblique angle; cut each of these to reverse the angle (a), because most cloths join better along the lengthwise threads than across the width. Pile up the strips of cloth one on top of the other, keeping them in order of cutting and all facing the same way. Now stitch them together on the sewing machine (b). There is no need to cut the cottons, just carry on from one join to the next, and when they are all sewn up snip through the cotton between each join (c). Trim the flanges of each join to about half their width. To flatten the seams, place each piece of piping on a clean hardwood block or a piece of flat iron and tap it with a broad-faced hammer (d). Or alternatively, press the joins with a hot iron and damp cloth. Roll the strip round a tube to keep it tidy and manageable (e) and from this it can be fed beneath your piping foot and folded evenly so that the edges are together (f).

Reupholstering the Chair Arms

This chair has scroll arm fronts (**fig. 86**); I have purposely used this sort as it is the most challenging. Other types of arms require less work.

First of all, temporarily replace the wing boards (**a**). Most modern wing chairs have rubberized hair pads on the arms. These must be re-padded. Firstly, lay on cotton felt. Place about three layers on the arm tops, but avoid too much bulk down the sides, as this would restrict the width of the seat (**b**).

Cut two pieces of 12 mm (½ in) polyether foam to the shape of the arms and two more pieces to the shape of the scroll fronts. Make these up like arm sleeves, joining the scroll-shaped ends into the ends of the larger pieces of foam with soft bond impact adhesive (**c**).

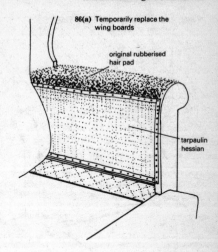

86(a) Temporarily replace the wing boards

original rubberised hair pad

tarpaulin hessian

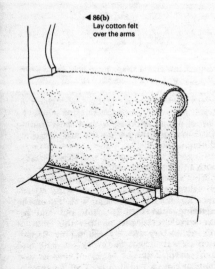

◀ 86(b) Lay cotton felt over the arms

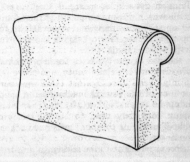

▼ 86(c) Make up arm sleeves in foam

Fig. 86 Re-upholstering the arms

▼ 86(d) Tighten the covering fabric round the periphery of the scroll

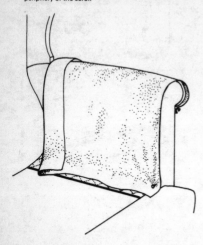

▼ 86(e) Fit and trim the scroll covering

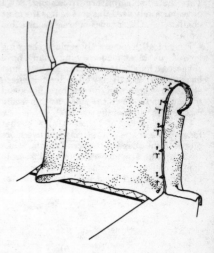

This makes a complete foam arm cover which can be fastened tightly with staples. If the two arm shapes are cut out together it will help to get the arms to the same shape.

Measure and cut off a piece of material to cover the main body of each arm and a piece to cover each front scroll. Position one of the arm covers over an arm, allowing 12 mm (½ in) to extend forward of the front scroll. Tighten the material round the periphery of the scroll, temporarily fastening it with tacks (d). Use small pins to pin a scroll cover to the arm cover that you have already positioned. Trim off the surplus material, then, to mark the position of the two pieces of fabric, nick or snip the seam flanges at intervals through the two thicknesses (e). Mark the first snip with a pen or chalk.

Remove this cover from the arm, take out the pins and lay the already trimmed pieces on top of the pieces for the other arm, right sides together. Trim the second set of covers to match, and also transfer the positioning snips. 'Make' the piping on to the two front shapes, allowing plenty of length at each end of the scroll.

Pin together the arm coverings and front

shapes, matching the positioning snips—now you see why it is necessary to mark the first snip. The pins should be on the front. Machine stitch the two pieces together, with the front scroll piece uppermost. Stitch just inside the row of piping stitches, so that these joining stitches do not show when the cover is turned the right side out.

Cover the whole of the arm foam surfaces with a thin layer of wadding.

You are now ready to put your made-up covering on, so remove those wing boards once again. It is quite simple to put on the covering—just turn it inside out and get the scroll positioned against the front of the upholstery (f), lay the piping flanges outwards then roll back the covering and tension towards the back, cutting in and tucking through as shown in (g). Fasten the cover to the back upright. Then fasten it at the bottom along the outside rail, and at the top beneath the roll over of the arm. I have shown the cutting in that is necessary before the final permanent tacking is done and you can see that the material is placed with wooden dowels protruding through holes made with a regulator.

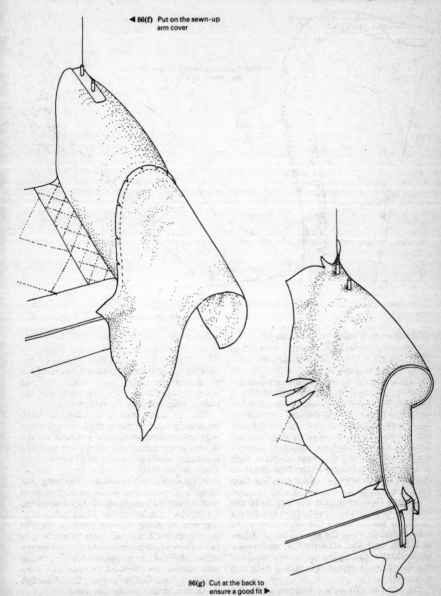

◄ 86(f) Put on the sewn-up arm cover

86(g) Cut at the back to ensure a good fit ►

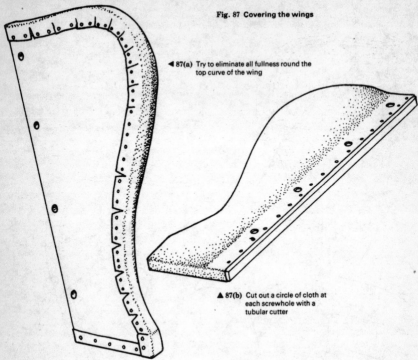

Fig. 87 Covering the wings

◀ 87(a) Try to eliminate all fullness round the top curve of the wing

▲ 87(b) Cut out a circle of cloth at each screwhole with a tubular cutter

Reupholstering the wings

Try the wing boards on the chair and note the space where each board touches the back upright. No padding is needed here. Also, while the boards are temporarily in position, mark a vertical line on the outside of each—this will give you a guide to help you get the covering on perfectly straight. Lay the boards flat and pad the inner surfaces with several layers of cotton felt. The shape of this upholstery is a matter for your personal choice; I like to see the wings well rounded but soft, with the filling feathering off on the top and front edges to define the curve of the wing (fig. 87).

Measure and cut off the pieces of fabric to cover the inner surfaces of the wings. Temporarily tack the cover to the inside of one wing board. Adjust the fabric until you have eliminated all fullness round the top curve and the gathers are neatly made on the outside (**a**). Make sure that the weave of the cloth is straight, then permanently tack the cover down. Cover the inner surface of the second wing board in the same way.

With a small tubular cutter or small scissors, cut out circles of cloth at each screw hole (**b**)—otherwise when the screws are put in they could catch and pull a thread in your material, making a nasty mark. Screw the wings in position.

Pin piping round the edge of the wings (**c**). Then pad the outer surfaces of the wing boards with a single layer of cotton wadding.

Cut the wing coverings roughly to shape and pin them in position close up to the piping (**d**). Tack the back edge down the rear facing side of the back upright and the bottom edge under the rail at the bottom of the wing. Sew round the curve of the top and front edges as described on page 43 in the section on incorporating piping into a seam.

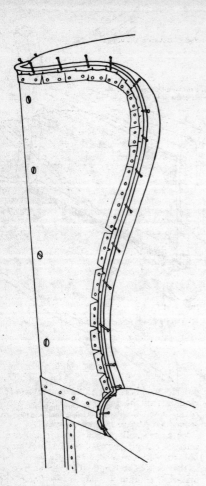

▲ 87(c) Pin piping round the edge of the wings

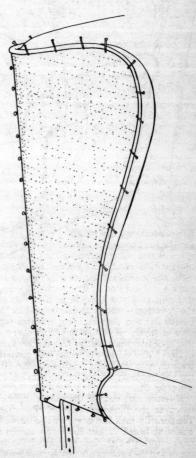

▼ 87(d) Pin the outside covering in position

Fig. 88 Covering the outside arm panels

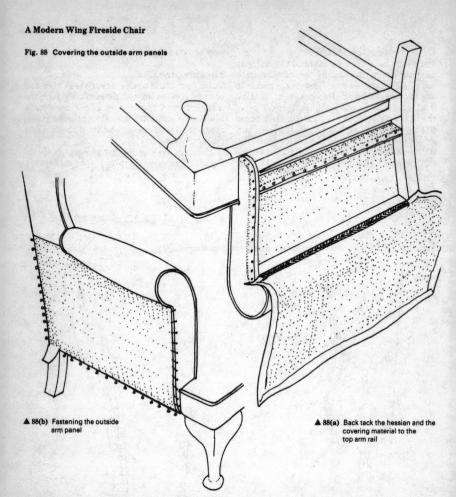

▲ 88(b) Fastening the outside arm panel

▲ 88(a) Back tack the hessian and the covering material to the top arm rail

Covering the Outside Arm Panels

Half a width of material will probably be enough to cover each outside arm panel (fig. 88). Measure and cut off the lengths required. Turn the chair upside down (a). Here you can see the covering material and a piece of 280 g (10 oz) support hessian fastened on to the arm rail using a 50 mm (2 in) wide strip of webbing folded in half down its length, stretched tightly along the length of the rail so that it sandwiches the edges of both the covering and the hessian. This webbing is fastened with 13 mm ($\frac{1}{2}$ in) Improved tacks at 25 mm (1 in) intervals. Care must be taken to keep the 'back tacking' straight and the webbing taut in order to keep the join close. Be careful—on some chairs the arm rails are not parallel with the seat rails below. Stretch the support hessian very tightly and fasten it round the outside of the chair frame. Tighten and temporarily fix the covering material under the bottom seat rail and down the rear of the back upright. Pin together the front seam (b), then ladder stitch it.

Covering the Outside Back

If a wing chair has a substantial top rail, you can back-tack the top of the outside back covering on to this rail. However, I prefer to see the top seam and the sides sewn, it takes a bit longer to do, but it makes a proper job of the upholstery. So pin the outside back panel to the side, arm and front covers and temporarily tack it on beneath the bottom rail (**fig. 89**). Ladder stitch (pages 40–41) the two upright seams and sew the top seam in the same way as you did on the wings.

Finishing the Chair

Turn your chair upside down again now and turn in, neaten off and permanently tack the material onto the bottom of the seat rails. Make nice straight lines of your turnings and space the tacks evenly so that it looks like a really professional job.

The final task is making the seat cushion. For directions, see Chapter 10 (pages 153–157).

Fig. 89 Covering the outside back

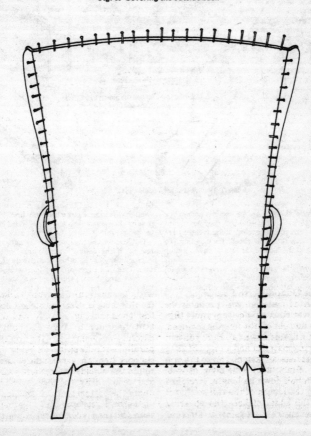

The previous chapters of this book cover most aspects of traditional upholstery, but occasionally you are sure to come across a chair, a stool or couch that has a peculiar feature of its own. It is these features, which entail deviations from the usual procedures, that I would like to include in this final chapter. So here, in alphabetical order, are some snippets of information on upholstery to help you with individual pieces.

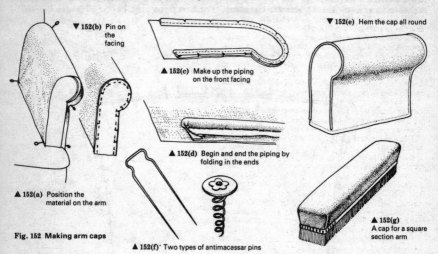

▼ 152(b)   Pin on the facing

▲ 152(c)   Make up the piping on the front facing

▼ 152(e)   Hem the cap all round

▲ 152(d)   Begin and end the piping by folding in the ends

▲ 152(a)   Position the material on the arm

Fig. 152   Making arm caps

▲ 152(f)˙   Two types of antimacassar pins

▲ 152(g)   A cap for a square section arm

ARM CAPS

Personally, I hate these loose protective covers for arms and I try to put people off when they ask me to make loose arm caps, for, in so many instances, they are never removed from the chair except for cleaning. To my mind they spoil the look of the arm, for even if they are well fitted they move about and require constant adjusting. And this fact of constant movement wears the permanent covering beneath to no little extent. But I am willing to admit that there are circumstances where they do prolong the good looks of a piece of upholstered furniture; mostly where it receives constant use, as in a hotel lounge or in the home of a large family.

Anyway, here are brief directions for making them up (**fig. 152**). If you have enough material, make the caps the full length of the arms and deep enough to tuck into the seat or cushion. If the covering cloth is patterned, it is nice to get the design to match in properly so that when they are on they look as inconspicuous as possible. This requires careful planning and measurement.

Measure and plan your cut so that the design matches that of the arm. Allow enough for hems on the top,

back and bottom edges—38 mm (1½ in) should be enough. Position a piece over one arm. Fasten it with pins or skewers at each end of the scroll edge, the back of the arm roll-over and the bottom back corner (**a**).

Cut the two facings so that the patterns are identical or, if the design demands this, so that one is a mirror image of the other. Pin one on the front of an arm. Trim the edges and cut positioning snips in the flanges through both thicknesses of cloth (**b**). Remove the cap, take out the pins and lay the two pieces of fabric face to face on the second arm cap pieces. Cut the second pieces to the same shape, duplicating the positioning snips (**c**).

Make piping on the edges of the two front facings (pages 82–84), starting and ending 50 mm (2 in) from the bottom (**d**). Fold in the ends of the piping. Pin, or tack with cotton, the fronts on to the main pieces, positioning the snips at the edges. Stitch the two pieces together with the scroll side uppermost. Keep just to the inside of the piping stitches. Zigzag or oversew the flanges of this piped seam.

To finish the arm caps, fold up and stitch a hem round the entire edge (**e**). You will now see why the piping was made to begin and finish 50 mm (2 in) from the ends.

It is no joke trying to sort out and fold over the piping in a hem. Use antimacassar pins (**f**) or small pieces of Velcro, sewn on where they cannot be seen (under the end of the roll-over of the arm and, perhaps, below the cushion line), to secure the arm caps.

These are the simplest form of arm caps; for some chairs more shaping and fitting may well be needed.

In (**g**) I have illustrated an example of a cap for a square section arm. This cap is trimmed with fringe.

ARM PADS

Upholstering an elbow rest or a padded top to an open or show wood arm involves a neat little intricate exercise in edge building (**fig. 153**).

I shall deal first with the arm rests of a Victorian spoon-back chair. To hold the horsehair, first fix a row of stuffing tie loops (page 44) down the centre of each platform with small tacks (**a**). The hair should be put on so that it consolidates to about 35 mm (1⅜ in) thick. Have plenty oversailing the edges of the platform, as the finished edges need to mushroom a little.

To ensure that the two pads are made the same size, cut identical pieces of scrim hessian and tack them on with the same amount of turn-under. Follow a thread of the weave with the rows of tacks on the sides.

When you come to stitch round the edges of the arm pads (pages 47–49), just one row of blind stitches above the line of tacks will be enough. Take care to avoid getting this upholstery lopsided. It is wise to put some temporary fixing, such as a row of 30 mm (1½ in) wire nails, down the centre of each pad before you stitch the roll (**b**). Hammer them in just far enough to hold the hessian while you are stitching the first side, the hessian is not pulled over by the stitches, thus causing the other side to be reduced in height. The nails can be removed when the edges are completed.

Put in more stuffing ties and add a thin layer of horsehair stuffing. Cover the arms with calico and then with two layers of cotton wadding. The arms are now ready for the top covering. Covering the arms pads is a fairly easy job, although it calls for a certain amount of dexterity with the fingers. It is best to stretch the covering over the arm pads lengthwise from back to front. In (**c**) you can see how to cut in to the centre of the arm show wood at the back and at the front: make two small oblique cuts to form a V to a little less than the width of the wood.

The corners of these arm covers are single pleated, in such a way that the open end of the pleats is facing to the front and back (**d**). In (**e**) a longer arm pad is shown and this time it is buttoned. The buttons are set out with the usual between-button allowance (page 102) and placed down the exact centre of the arm, and the material is pleated across the width at each button. Special buttons are made for this sort of arm, with long wire nail shanks instead of the usual wire loop or calico extrusions. The shanks are pushed through the upholstery and hammered into the woodwork beneath. However, it is possible to use ordinary buttons and fasten them with twine. With the aid of a large curved needle you can bring the twine out at each side of the edge and fix it with tacks before the material is pleated and fastened.

Fig. 153 Re-upholstering arm pads

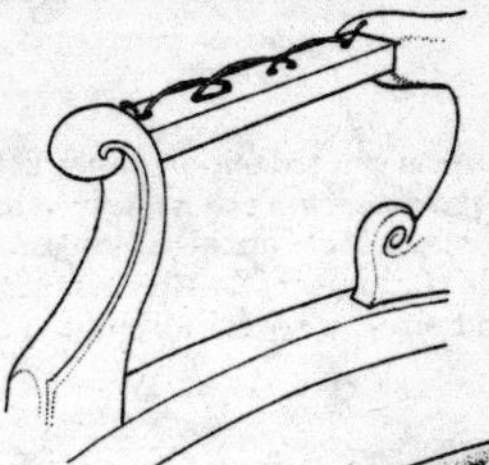

◀ 153(a)
Put in stuffing ties to hold the horsehair

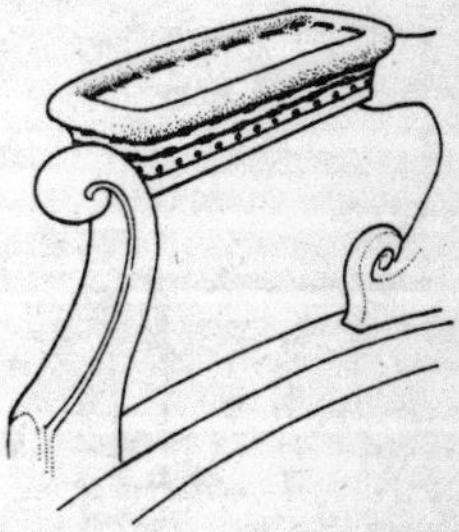

153(b) ▶
Make the roll edge

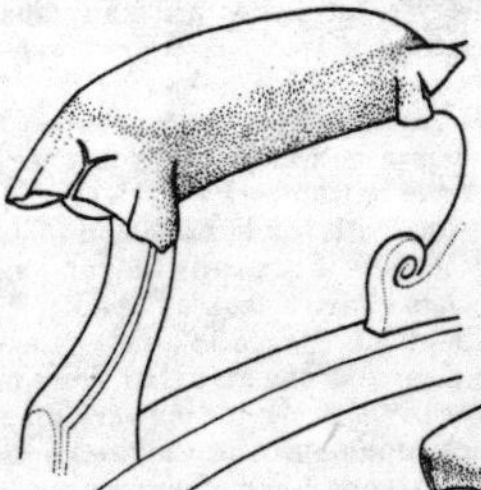

◀ 153(c)
Cover the arm pad

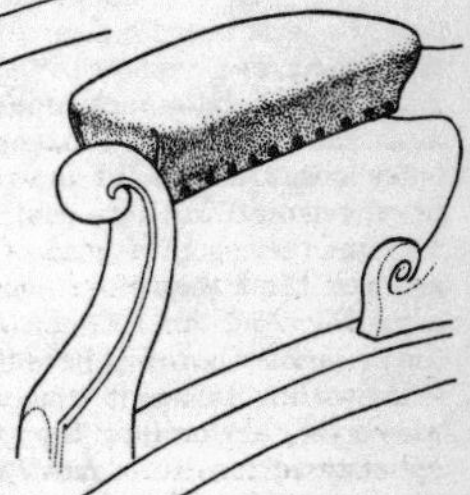

153(d) ▶
Make single pleats at the corners

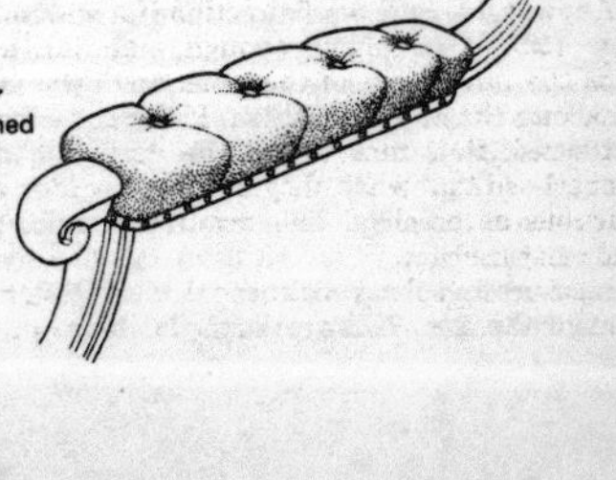

153(e) ▶
A buttoned arm pad

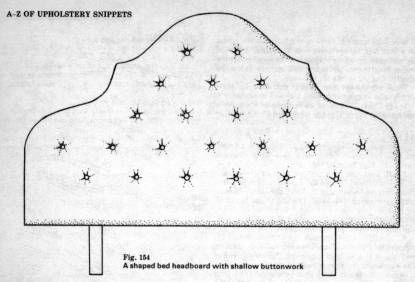

Fig. 154
A shaped bed headboard with shallow buttonwork

BED HEADS
The designs for upholstered bed heads are many and varied. Here are just a few.

Deep-Buttoned Headboards
Deep-buttoning a headboard is a most rewarding job, because on a flat board the buttonwork can be set out and executed to perfection, with the buttons and folds precisely placed. The procedure is basically the same as for any deep buttonwork, so have a look at Chapter 7, (pages 102–107) and Chapter 9, (pages 142–144). However, the back board has none of the give that there is with the hessian support beneath the buttonwork on a chair or settee. Here is a rough guide to the thickness of padding needed for an average depth of buttons.

If you use polyether foam (this must, of course, be flame-resistant), cut a piece of 25 mm (1 in) thickness to the exact shape of the board—place the headboard on top of the foam and cut round it with a very sharp knife. Then cut from 12 mm ($\frac{1}{2}$ in) sheet foam a piece that is larger than the board by 50 mm (2 in) all round and stretch and shape this piece of foam over the 25 mm (1 in) layer. Taking the 12 mm ($\frac{1}{2}$ in) sheet foam over in this way softens the edges. With your tubular cutter, cut holes at each of the button positions, right through the two layers of foam.

If you use acrylic wool, pad the board with a thickness of about 50 mm (2 in), then stretch over a layer of 6 mm ($\frac{1}{4}$ in) foam, cut holes just through the foam then part a way right through the wool with two fingers. A little reminder here: always overlay the foam with some cotton wadding.

These are the quick ways of deep buttoning. If you wish to upholster your bed head in the classic way, using horsehair and making stitched roll edges all round (see pages 47–49), make the head up to a depth of about 50 mm (2 in). When it comes to covering, make the edge borders separately. You can trim with piping, cord or braid.

Period Headboards
A period headboard with a padded panel contained within a polished, painted or gilded show wood frame is usually easy to refurbish, as most panels can be removed for padding and covering. When the panel is replaced the tacks are concealed within the outer frame. The backs of these, and indeed any upholstered headboards, should always be lined with calico or a lining cloth. The padding for a plain headboard can be of cotton felt, cotton wadding, polyether or latex foam, or, for a very rich and soft padding, acrylic wool.

One word of warning: when covering something plain and flat, do beware of making tack marks or tack pulls, especially on thin and delicate fabrics. If cloth is stretched too tightly, the tension at the site of the tack head will make a distinct line over the surface of the work. The solution is to keep tension to the maximum laterally along the edges, and to the minimum across the work. And, again, corner to corner diagonal stretching is important in achieving this. Of course, you must also be careful, when putting tacks in, not to snag a thread in the weave.

Shaped Headboards with Shallow Buttonwork
Headboards of the type shown in **fig. 154** are usually thinly padded. The buttons, which are placed without any prior setting out or folding of the covering, are held by twine pulled through holes bored through the wood. Plain boards like these look good covered in stretchy vinyl leathercloth over a 38 mm ($1\frac{1}{2}$ in) padding of foam. When the buttons are pulled in evenly the effect is very pleasing.

'BIBLE' CHAIR EDGES

A few Victorian easy chairs have shaped seats with fronts in the form of a large roll resembling the rounded spine of a book. These are known as 'bible' edges (fig. 155a).

In (b) you can see how the bible edge is built. The two sides or ends are stitched up with blind rows of edge stitches and a roll edge is made to define the rounded shape (pages 47–49). Great care must be taken to get the two sides to the same size and shape. After the sides have been finished a loose row of through stitches is put in to hold the filling within the roll (page 97). The top stuffing should be thinly laid so that the book spine shape is retained.

BOX INTERIORS

Relining a box interior is another task that the upholsterer is expected to be able to do, so I will try to help with a few notes and pictures of the methods used. Most of it, though, is fairly straightforward—really just a matter of common sense.

Relining a Trinket Box

We have decided to line this trinket box in delicate silk (fig. 156). You will need some thin cardboard (ticket board) which is fairly stiff—this can be purchased at a stationer's shop—and some slow-setting impact adhesive, preferably the easy to spread thixotropic kind.

Fig. 155 Reupholstering a 'bible' chair edge

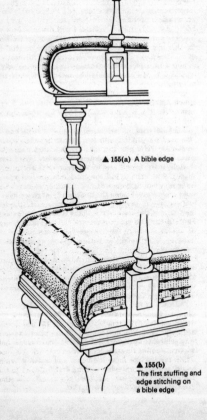

▲ 155(a) A bible edge

▲ 155(b)
The first stuffing and edge stitching on a bible edge

Fig. 156 Re-lining a trinket box

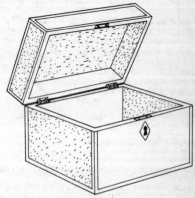

▲ 156(a) Trinket box ready for re-lining

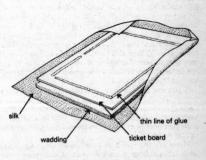

silk

wadding

thin line of glue

ticket board

▲ 156(b) Ticket board, wadding and silk cut ready for gluing of the panel

▼ 156(c) The three layers of the panel carefully glued together for fastening inside the box

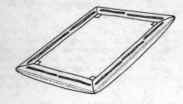

▼ 156(d) Miniature buttoning

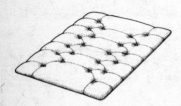

Clean the inside of the box thoroughly, removing all the old lining, glue and dirt. Carefully cut and fit pieces of ticket board as panels for the sides, the top and the floor of the box; these should be a loose fit to allow for the thickness of the lining (b). Each panel can be padded with a thin layer of cotton wadding or acrylic wool and covered with your silk. When all the panels have been covered they can be fastened to the inside of the box with just a line of glue near the edges of each panel—but not so near that it will squeeze out and show (c).

If you use a panel of slightly thicker card for lining the inside of the lid, you will be able to pad and decorate it in various ways; for instance, you can set out some miniature buttoning using French knots instead of buttons (d) (page 36), or random gather the material to give a crumpled appearance.

Covering and Lining a Box Ottoman

Large boxes such as ottoman chests or box ottomans or, larger still, ottoman divans, are, you will probably find, even easier to reline than smaller boxes, as they are less fiddly (fig. 157). In this section I will describe how to line a box ottoman. I will ignore the lid/seat upholstery, for this has been dealt with in the chapter on stuffed-over seats (pages 68–73). However, although this section is about linings I must mention the outside covering of the box, as this is closely integrated with the relining.

In many ottomans the base boards are removable, which makes covering and lining much easier. I will assume that you have removed the base board and completely stripped your ottoman (a).

If the material you are using has a bit of stretch to it, you can make up the outside covering in panels to the sizes of the sides plus turnings, stitch them together on a machine and pull the whole over the box. With non-stretchy material it is best to cover each side separately. Also, if you want to pad the outside of the box with a layer of wadding you will find it easier to cover the sides separately. Fasten the back and front coverings as you see in (b), tacking the covers just inside the top inside rim of the box and round the corners at the sides. Then fit the two side covers and ladder stitch (pages 40–41) the seams at the corners. Leave the bottom unfastened—you have the bottom boards to put back, remember.

Now, using thin strips of cardboard, back-tack the lining over the flange of the outside cover inside the top of the box (c). The strips of cardboard are used in the same way as webbing is employed for covering the outside arms of a wing fireside chair (page 88).

Pad each of the inner sides with a layer of wadding and then stretch over the lining and fasten it under the bottom edge of the wood. Line the two longer sides first, stretching the lining sideways, then cover the two shorter sides. Turn in the fabric at the corners and ladder stitch the seams together (d).

Pad and line the base and board and fasten it to the box. Stretch the outside covering and fasten it to the underside of the box (e). Lastly, put on a bottom covering of lining, hessian or calico.

Fig. 157 Covering and lining a box ottoman

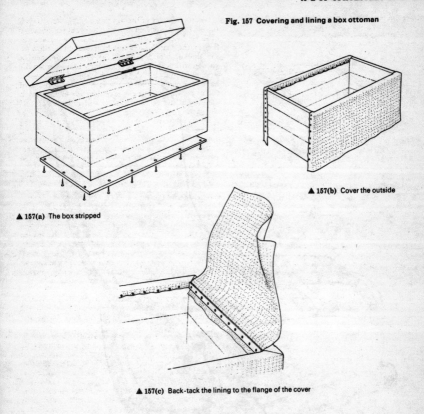

▲ 157(a) The box stripped

▲ 157(b) Cover the outside

▲ 157(c) Back-tack the lining to the flange of the cover

157(d) A view of the box with one side removed

157(e) Re-fix the base board and fasten the cover to the bottom

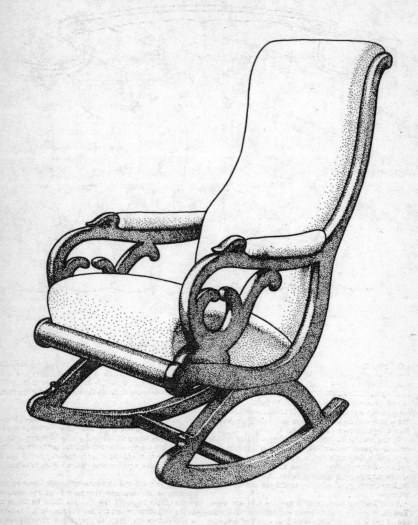

Fig. 158 A Victorian rocking chair with a removable box seat

Fig. 159 An alternative way of setting out buttonwork

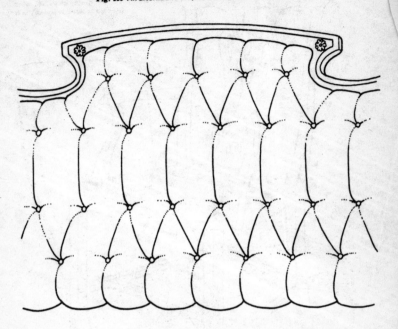

BOX SEATS

Deeply sprung removable 'box' seats are to be found in some Victorian show wood easy chairs, such as the rocking chair illustrated in **fig. 158**. There are two ways of upholstering these box seats. The easier way is to keep the springs to the centre of the seat frame and lace them into a domed shape, then build up the edges to form a high edge with a roll (pages 47–49).

In the second method the springs are kept to the outside edges of the seat frame, edged with spring steel wire and laced into a flat box shape. The springs are then covered with heavy hessian and securely fastened to the springs with twine stitches. A first stuffing is built up, with a roll edge, on to the top of this spring platform.

A box seat can be covered in various different ways. You can make a complete cover and pull it over. Or the top of the seat can be covered first and the covering fastened under the lip of the roll edge with blind stitches. The border is then ladder stitched (pages 40–41) on by hand. Or a stuffed border can be made with

piping or chair cord and recessed in just beneath the roll edge. At each stage of the upholstery the seat should be tried in the chair to make sure that it still fits—it is very easy to make the sides too bulky to fit in.

BUTTONWORK

The picture in **fig. 159** of the back of a show wood settee illustrates a variation in buttoning—a style which incorporates straight, vertical pleats between rows of buttons in a diamond formation. This method was often used in carriage and early car upholstery and it can be used on settees, couches and chairs which have rather high backs.

When you set out the measurements between the buttons at the top and the bottom of the vertical pleats (pages 102–107), the distance must be the same on the upholstery as on the back of the cloth. No extra is allowed on the cloth, so that when covering takes place the vertical pleats can be tucked well down into the upholstery and held tightly between the buttons at the top and the bottom.

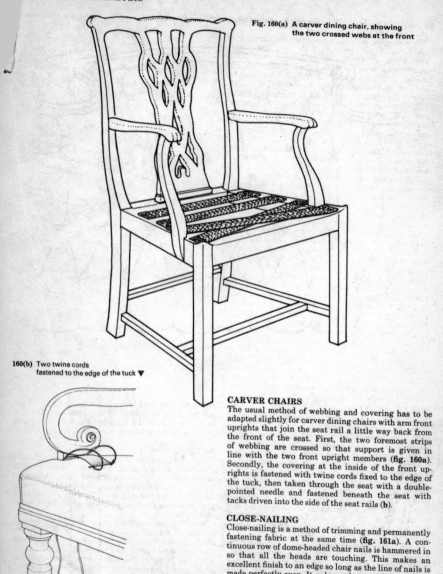

Fig. 160(a) A carver dining chair, showing the two crossed webs at the front

160(b) Two twine cords fastened to the edge of the tuck ▼

CARVER CHAIRS

The usual method of webbing and covering has to be adapted slightly for carver dining chairs with arm front uprights that join the seat rail a little way back from the front of the seat. First, the two foremost strips of webbing are crossed so that support is given in line with the two front upright members (**fig. 160a**). Secondly, the covering at the inside of the front uprights is fastened with twine cords fixed to the edge of the tuck, then taken through the seat with a double-pointed needle and fastened beneath the seat with tacks driven into the side of the seat rails (**b**).

CLOSE-NAILING

Close-nailing is a method of trimming and permanently fastening fabric at the same time (**fig. 161a**). A continuous row of dome-headed chair nails is hammered in so that all the heads are touching. This makes an excellent finish to an edge so long as the line of nails is made perfectly even. It only needs a couple of nails to be slightly out of place to ruin the whole effect. The size of chair nail most used in upholstery has a 12 mm (½ in) shank, with a 10 mm (⅜ in) diameter head, but larger and smaller nails can be obtained.

When buying chair nails, do not get the cheaper sort, which are brass plated on steel. The thin brass plating soon wears off and the nails begin to rust. Better quality nails have solid brass dome heads with steel shanks. You can buy them in three finishes: polished brass, and light and dark antique brass. Where possible, I prefer the light antique finish to the polished brass, which soon becomes dull and lack-lustre. The dark antique nails sometimes have a greyish look like gun-metal. Of course, which of these finishes is most suitable will depend on the colour of your furnishing fabric.

Close-nailing does have a disadvantage in that the close row of shanks tends to perforate the wood along the grain and some woods, such as oak, may then split open along this line.

The trained upholsterer will close-nail very accurately just by eye, judging distance and straightness without measuring aids. But I would recommend for beginners a simply made guide and gauge for positioning chair nails. Teddy, who lives next door to my workshop, is always full of bright ideas, and it was when I suggested that he might trim the dining chair seat that he was reupholstering with domed chair nails instead of braid that he turned his inventive mind to making a guide for spacing the nails accurately. Here is a picture of it (**b**). It is just a bent strip of fairly thick aluminium in which a slot has been cut. The width of the guide is exactly the diameter of the nail head. The slot is filed out so that the shank of the nail is an easy fit and is the length of the radius of the nail head, plus a little extra to allow for the thickness of the shank. If this guide is placed against the edge of the show wood or level with the bottom of the seat rail, a nail can be placed in the slot and hammered home. The guide is then placed close up to this first nail head to give the exact distance for placing the next nail so that the heads just touch. This aid will enable you to achieve a professional look with little skill—but don't rely on it all the time; occasionally try nailing by eye as the real professionals do.

Fig. 161 Close-nailing

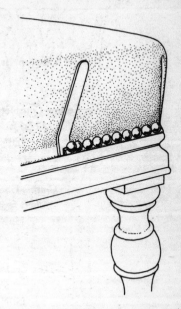

161(b) A simple gauge for close-nailing

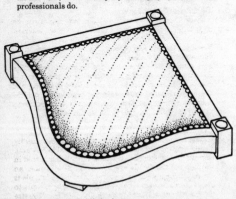

161(a) A close-nailed chair edge

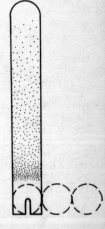

Other titles from HarperCollins*Publishers* include

Collins Complete Woodworker's Manual
Albert Jackson and David Day
ISBN 0 00 411565 1
Price: £24.99

Collins Good Wood Handbook
Albert Jackson and David Day
ISBN 0 00 412560 6
Price: £9.99

The Craftsman Woodturner
Peter Child
ISBN 0 00 412686 6
Price: £14.99